362.83
Ise   Isenberg, Sheila

           Women who love
           men who kill

WITHDRAWN

DUE DATE

WOMEN
WHO LOVE

MEN WHO KILL

Sheila Isenberg

Simon & Schuster

NEW YORK   LONDON   TORONTO   SYDNEY   TOKYO   SINGAPORE

Simon & Schuster
Simon & Schuster Building
Rockefeller Center
1230 Avenue of the Americas
New York, New York 10020

SIMON & SCHUSTER and colophon are registered trademarks
of Simon & Schuster Inc.
Designed by Carla Weise/Levavi & Levavi
Manufactured in the United States of America

1   3   5   7   9   10   8   6   4   2

Library of Congress Cataloging-in-Publication Data
Isenberg, Sheila.
Women who love men who kill / Sheila Isenberg.
p.   cm.
Includes bibliographical references.
1. Murderers—United States—Family relationships—Case studies.
2. Prisoners' wives—United States—Psychology—Case studies.
3. Attachment behavior—United States—Case studies.   4. Co-
dependence (Psychology)—United States—Case studies.   5. Love—
Psychological aspects—Case studies.   I. Title.
HV6529.I74   1991   90-28130
362.8'3—dc20   CIP

ISBN 0-671-70247-5

Excerpt (to be used as an epigraph) from *Holy the Firm* by
Annie Dillard. Copyright © 1977 by Annie Dillard. Reprinted
by permission of Harper & Row, Publishers, Inc.

Acknowledgments

Finding answers to questions about women who love men who kill has been a long but exciting quest, one I could not have undertaken without the help of many people. My mainstay throughout this process has been my husband— always supportive, optimistic, and willing to listen, read, and reread. I am very grateful to my daughter for giving me the gift of a peaceful year. My deepest thanks to my agent, Richard Curtis, for his support and encouragement; to my editor, Susanne Jaffe, for her incisive shaping of the manuscript; to my friend Jed Horne, whose reading of the manuscript and suggestions were invaluable; and to the Radical Debutantes for their love and support.

I am deeply grateful to the numerous professionals in psychiatry, psychology, social work, criminology, and journalism who helped and advised: Neil Kaye, M.D.; Park Elliott Dietz, M.D.; Janet Warren, DSW; Emanuel Tanay, M.D.; Jane Caputi, Ph.D.; Carl Rotenberg, M.D.; Streamson Chua, M.D.; Charlotte Kasl, Ph.D.; Michael Baden, M.D.; Abe Halpern, M.D.; Joseph Faulkner, Jr., MSW, whose thesis was the only dissertation I found on the subject; reporters Diane Albright, Angela Aiello, and Pat Plarski; Lt. Cammy Voss at Folsom Prison; and FBI Supervisory Special Agent William Hagmaier. My thanks also to colleague and friend Joan Byalin, to Helene Weinstein for her patience, to computer wizard Sarah Beaver, and to librarian extraordinaire Judy Fischetti. I am also very grateful to the many other individuals too numerous to name who graciously took the time to return phone calls, look up information, and patiently answer my endless questions.

Finally, my deepest gratitude goes to the many women who shared their stories. This book is possible only because of them

For my father

Contents

Author's Preface

As a news junkie and former reporter, I follow certain news items with great interest, always seeking the story behind the story. During late 1987 and 1988, Joseph Pikul, a successful Wall Street analyst suspected of having murdered his second wife, Diane, was much in the news. The story heated up when Pikul, to the dismay of many, was awarded temporary custody of his two young children. Headlines sizzled when Pikul remarried and his third wife, Mary Bain—blond, attractive, twenty years his junior—testified during a custody hearing that he'd slashed her dress with a hunting knife.

When I first read that Mary Bain had left her husband and young daughter to live with Pikul and his children, I became intrigued. Why did she marry a man charged with murder? Wasn't she afraid? Then, after he slashed her dress, why didn't she leave him? Mary told a *Newsday* reporter that she couldn't "walk away" from love, and on television's "A Current Affair," she described how much she loved Pikul. But *why* did she love him? He didn't appear particularly handsome or charismatic. He was about to stand trial for murder. What did Mary see in Pikul? Was there something within her that made her want to get involved, to take on his cause?

Mary's romance with Pikul reminded me of another woman in love with a murderer, Naomi Zack. Zack's husband, the notorious murderer and jailhouse author Jack Henry Abbott, was on parole for a prison murder when he stabbed a man to death in 1981. Abbott was doing time in an upstate New York prison when Naomi became involved with him. She left her hometown and family to live near his prison. A Ph.D. in philosophy from Columbia University, Naomi was intelligent and talented. What was it about Abbott that attracted her? He had spent his life in institutions, had committed a murder only weeks after he was released, and might, one could easily assume, murder again. I had heard that Naomi was passionately in love with Abbott and viewed him as a hero, not a criminal. I wanted to know why.

As a reporter, I had often seen women in prison visiting rooms, waiting patiently to see their husbands or boyfriends. How many of those inmates were in for murder? Of the women in love with murderers, had they fallen in love *after* the man's conviction? If so, how did they meet?

Were these women the most passionate women of all, who would not allow even prison walls to separate them from their lovers? Were they thrill seekers? Did they find it erotic and exciting to be involved with killers? Were they damaged individuals, seeking a continuation of their pain?

I wondered: Is it possible that the men who commit an "arbitrary, sordid, pathetic, and ugly" crime such as murder—in the words of writer P. D. James—can be lovable, attractive, and desirable? Or is their beauty solely in the eyes of the beholder?

Since the murderers we hear the most about are those who end up behind bars, it seemed that these women were also reacting to the prison situation; they wanted a relationship with an inmate. But would any convict do? Did women also fall for burglars, white-collar criminals, drug dealers? Or was it only murderers who drew them? If so, why? Was it something in their pasts that led them to love men who had killed?

When I started looking for answers to these questions, I found there weren't any. No one had examined the phenomenon of women who love murderers. Everyone knew about these women and questioned their motives, but no one had tried to understand those motives. Police, attorneys, and prison officials were all too familiar with prison groupies. Forensic psychiatrists and social workers, who study the behavior of murderers, were well aware that many were attractive to women and formed relationships after they were convicted.

But no one knew what proportion of convicted murderers attracted women. And no one knew anything about those women. Psychiatrists and psychologists have been too busy studying the murderers themselves. It is only now that they are starting to look at murderers' relationships in hopes they'll shed some light on their behavior and motives.

Apparently my curiosity is timely. As I finished the manuscript, the movie *Miami Blues* was released. Its plot pivots on the relationship between a charming con-man murderer and a woman who wants to believe he is really a knight in shining armor. And forensic social worker Janet Warren, DSW, like many other professionals I interviewed, said she believed it was time for specialists to look closely at the relationships between murderers and their women—a "crossover," she calls it, between criminology and psychology.

Using techniques I learned as a reporter, I managed to find dozens of women all over the country who were in love with murderers. I realized it would be impossible to talk to anyone involved with a murderer who was not yet convicted. Indeed, I was not able to interview Mary Bain Pikul until her husband's trial was just about over. So I limited my interviews only to those women in love with men already convicted of murder. Surprisingly, they were not hard to find.

While many women were eager to talk about their relationships and their pasts, others were reluctant, saying they didn't want to hurt their men's cases. The women who agreed to be interviewed were gracious, helpful, talking intimately about their childhoods, past relationships, values, lifestyles—and about the men they love.

These women live a difficult life, a life on the edge, never knowing whether or when they will actually be with their men. But that, I have discovered, is a large part of the attraction. The women, damaged in many ways, have a deep need to love someone with whom they *can't* enjoy an easy, comfortable relationship.

In this book, you will meet these women and the murderers they love. For the purposes of confidentiality, I've altered many names, locations, and other identifying elements. In certain cases, this disguising of elements extends to newspapers used as sources.

I also interviewed psychiatrists, psychologists, district attorneys, police, and prison officials. And in some cases, I visited the murderers themselves in prison or exchanged letters with them.

Although I've developed a profile of women who love men who murder, this is not a scientific study. The profile described here is not intended to represent all women in this group. But I believe enough women have been interviewed at length to give a fairly accurate picture. It is my hope this book will stimulate further study in this area.

Introduction

Criminals and criminal acts fascinate most everyone. People enjoy playing armchair detective, speculating on the motive behind some dastardly crime reported in the news. Perhaps this fascination arises because most of us are indeed quite capable of such acts ourselves, sometimes even imagining ourselves the perpetrator. What separates us from the real criminals is likely our good behavior, respect for the law, and fear of punishment.

In *Women Who Love Men Who Kill,* Sheila Isenberg has used her background as an investigative reporter to locate and interview women whose fascination with murderers goes beyond the ordinary. She presents us with in-depth and personal information from women who have developed intimate relationships with convicted killers. She takes the reader on a journey into the psychiatric, psychologic, and sociologic factors that lead these women to their men. With vivid descriptions and often in the women's own words, she affords the reader a unique view of the special lives these women live.

Forensic psychiatry is the application of psychiatric knowledge and principles to the law for legal purposes. Most often, forensic psychiatry is known for its presence in criminal matters.

A forensic psychiatrist may become involved in criminal litigation and may be called upon during a trial. Issues to be addressed include competency to stand trial, criminal responsibility for the alleged act (insanity defense), aid in sentencing, and care and treatment issues for prisoners or those found not criminally responsible.

Training for a forensic psychiatrist involves five years of study after medical school. After another two years of practice, a forensic psychiatrist may sit for the specialized National Board Examination in Forensic Psychiatry.

During this training, each individual spends countless hours interviewing, treating, and working with criminals. My personal training included work in county jails, state prisons, and maximum-security state mental hospitals. In doing so, I have had the chance to meet personally the men that you, the reader, will meet through the eyes of their wives. In addition, I, too, have had the opportunity to meet some of the women Sheila Isenberg describes.

I am impressed by the abundance of material the author has acquired and developed for the reader. I know of no other person who has interviewed as many women in this position. Largely, the scientific community has been so engrossed in studying the criminal mind in an effort to be able to predict and thus to prevent future violence that little study has been done of women who marry murderers. This is undoubtedly a shame as these women may indeed provide a new window through which to view these men and might well lead to a better understanding of why men murder. Certainly, it is my hope that this book will stimulate more serious scientific research in this area.

In *Women Who Love Men Who Kill*, Sheila Isenberg has made a formidable effort to profile for the reader some of the characteristics of these women. Her skills as a reporter and interviewer of these women are keen; this, coupled with the extensive time she has spent with experts in the field, has enabled her to develop her thesis of who these women are.

The book includes a look at the roles of victimization, fantasy, the sexual aspects of violence, identification with the murderer, salvation and reforming, substitution, denial, father replacements, devotion, and the desperate need to fill the emptiness in these women's lives.

The conclusions she reaches are poignant and undoubtedly valid. Just as no one can accurately identify a future killer, neither can one identify the woman who will later choose to love and/or marry a killer. However, Sheila Isenberg goes a long way toward understanding why these women are so especially sensitive to the personality traits commonly seen in men who murder. These include superficial charm, sharp intelligence, and extreme egocentricity. She makes it possible for the reader to experience some of the emotional excitement these women feel when they are with "their men."

The author has very successfully put into words the knowledge she has gleaned from devoting two years of her life to interviewing women who love and marry murderers. *Women Who Love Men Who Kill* is riveting, personal, and revealing. Because all of the material is from actual, live cases, it is captivating for the reader. It will be enjoyed by everyone, whether lay or professional.

Neil S. Kaye, M.D.
Forensic Psychiatrist
Medical Center of Delaware

One night a moth flew into the candle, was caught, burnt dry, and held. . . . A golden female moth, a biggish one with a two-inch wingspan, flapped into the fire, dropped her abdomen into the wet wax, stuck, flamed, frazzled and fried in a second. . . .

And then this moth-essence, this spectacular skeleton, began to act as a wick. She kept burning. The wax rose in the moth's body from her soaking abdomen to her thorax to the jagged hole where her head should be, and widened into flame. . . .

She burned for two hours without changing, without bending or leaning—only glowing within, like a building fire glimpsed through silhouetted walls, like a hollow saint, like a flame-faced virgin gone to God.

—*Annie Dillard*
Holy the Firm

Maria: A Case of Identification

"He came from a good family"

THE HALLOWEEN MURDERER

At almost four years of age, Niki was old enough to go trick-or-treating. For weeks, with the help of her mother, Tina, she'd tried to decide whether to go as Miss Piggy or a witch. Tina, twenty-three, was trying to break up with her boyfriend, Phil Sylvester, so she only half-listened to Niki's chatter.

A week before Halloween, 1977, a week before the night her mother would be murdered, Niki finally decided she would masquerade as a witch. Tina cut holes in a sheet for Niki's blue eyes, her tiny nose and mouth. On the morning of October 31, Tina bought a broom and a pointy witch's hat in the Philadelphia suburb where she and Niki lived with Phil. It was the last purchase she ever made.

Waiting innocently for night to fall, the little girl ran around her apartment, her costume over her jeans and T-

21

shirt. Her mother yelled at her to be quiet. Phil put her bodily into her room and told her to stay there.

It seemed to the little girl that Phil was angry a lot of the time. Phil and Tina had shouting brawls at all hours of the day and night; the neighbors, disturbed by the noise, would bang on the walls until the racket stopped.

Tina, slender and five feet eight inches tall with long brown hair, was described by the building superintendent as beautiful. She had lived in the apartment in Wynnefield Terrace for two years, alone with her daughter, after she and her husband separated.

Phil, twenty-two, came from a large family—nine brothers and sisters—but he spent much of his adolescence, from the age of fourteen on, in the streets. A devil-may-care attitude combined with a handsome face and a muscular body made him enormously appealing to girls.

Days after he and Tina met, they began living together. But only two months later, Tina, strung out on drugs and drinking too much, decided she was tired of Phil; she wanted him out. The fighting began in earnest then. Phil was a Don Juan, a manipulator and controller of women whose ego couldn't accept that he was being kicked out. None of his other girlfriends had broken up with him; he had done the leaving.

Tina was afraid of Phil because he had abused her physically, and that was, in part, why she wanted to end the relationship. Tina's rejection hurt and enraged Phil. For him, apparently, as with other people with certain emotional problems, "the crime of abandonment is so obscene that it must be punished by death," wrote psychiatrist Emanuel Tanay, M.D., in *The Murderers*.

At four-thirty P.M. that Halloween Monday, Niki's father arrived to take her trick-or-treating in the nearby Philadelphia neighborhood where he lived. Tina kissed Niki good-bye for the last time. Sometime before seven P.M., Phil returned home, bringing a friend with him. Earlier that day, Phil had displayed a .38-caliber revolver and loaded it in the presence of some friends. That evening, as soon as Phil entered the apartment, he and Tina began fighting. After he hustled her into the bedroom, leaving his friend in the living room, the fight escalated.

After about fifteen minutes of shouting and loud bangs and crashes, Phil's friend heard a gunshot. He ran into the bedroom and saw Tina on the bed, the side of her face blown off. Phil stood there, the pearl-handled .38 still in his hand.

Phil and the other man ran from the apartment but then separated. Phil returned to a rented room he kept in a suburb, Havertown, about twenty minutes away.

Although Tina's neighbors liked her and thought her "very attractive" and "very nice," none of them had ever called the police during her shouting matches with Phil. The gunshot was something else. Police received an anonymous phone call from a neighbor and within minutes were at the apartment.

The neighborhood was filled with small figures in costumes, trick-or-treating, as police cars, sirens whining, pulled up to Tina's apartment building shortly after seven. Across town, little Niki was happily putting Tootsie Rolls and candy corn into her shopping bag as she and her father made their way door-to-door.

Smashing in the door to the apartment, the police found Tina lying across a bed. She died of a gunshot wound angled upward into her brain. Tina was wearing jeans, a black blouse with red flowers embroidered on the cuffs and collar, and a red turtleneck framing what was left of her beautiful face.

The morning editions of some Philadelphia papers dubbed Phil Sylvester, the prime suspect, "the Halloween Murderer." The following afternoon, accompanied by his brother, he gave himself up to Lower Merion Township and Philadelphia police. No stranger to the Philadelphia justice system, Sylvester had a prior burglary conviction so was held without bail for a November hearing. The following April, he stood trial for murder.

Two key witnesses testified that Sylvester, on that fateful Halloween, had showed them a snub-nosed .38 with a two-inch barrel and pearl handle. Sylvester claimed he didn't know the gun was loaded and that the shooting was unintentional; his defense attorney argued the gun had gone off accidentally. But the Commonwealth of Pennsylvania produced a similar weapon, and over defense counsel's objection, the prosecution's ballistics expert used it to demonstrate that considerable pressure must be exerted to pull the trigger on that particular type of gun.

During Sylvester's trial, the Commonwealth argued that Tina had been strangled and slapped across the mouth just before she was shot. Barbara Christie, chief of the Homicide Unit in the Philadelphia District Attorney's Office, said Sylvester showed her how he did it: "He strangled her with one hand, and at the same time he was shooting her with the other hand. . . . He had the barrel of the gun pressed up against her. . . . I asked him to demonstrate. He was a big guy, a very big guy, with big hands. She was slender."

The nature of the wound and the powder burns on Tina's skin proved that, at the time the fatal shot was fired, Phil was holding the gun against her cheek.

After six days of testimony, jurors quickly reached a verdict of guilty; they did not believe the shooting was accidental. One month later, Phil was sentenced to life in prison. Barring a miracle, Phil Sylvester, twenty-three, ladies' man, would spend the rest of his days in a steel and concrete building with other men convicted of society's most violent crimes.

Five years after the steel doors clanged shut behind him, Phil Sylvester would meet his salvation—a woman who would love him unconditionally, bring him warmth and affection, and once again convince him that he was handsome, sexy, irresistible—a man women loved to love. Maria Califano, buxom, black haired, brimming over with femininity and sensuality, would bring to Phil Sylvester the worshipful love he needed so desperately. And he, in turn, would give her the attention and affection she craved.

On the day Phil murdered Tina, Maria was working with preschool children in Youngstown, Ohio. Almost the same age as Phil but far less worldly, Maria would provide Phil with a link to the outside world, protect him from the dehumanization of prison, and promise him a sensual and sexual heaven in her arms—if he ever gained his freedom.

MARIA'S STORY

Maria was born in Youngstown, the oldest of six children in a close-knit, Catholic family. It fell to her to act as dutiful, surrogate mother to her five younger brothers when their mother was working and their father, although home, was unavailable because he was doing "men's work," like repairing old cars or cleaning up the yard.

Maria was considered a tomboy in the blue-collar neighborhood where she grew up; she had to be tough enough to protect her younger brothers. She gained value and self-esteem as their caretaker and protector. As a girl, the only worth she had was as nurturer, as bodyguard for the littler boys, as second mother.

Although Maria recalls a "happy childhood," she was afraid of her parents. She was hit, but not abused. However, when she received a failing grade in one high school subject, she was "scared to death" to go home.

As she got older, she grew frustrated with her household responsibilities. "I resented the fact that I had to come home from school and take care of my brothers. . . . Part of my sixteenth birthday present was that I didn't have to wash dishes anymore . . . and they gave me a key to the house." Finally, at sixteen, Maria was accepted, the key a message from her parents that she belonged. She described her parents as "strict and overprotective," warning her not to date or ride around in cars. She had no sexual relationships as a teenager.

But as she grew from a teenager into a young woman, Maria began to experiment sexually, and her experiences

were mainly disasters. A supervisor sexually harassed her at
one of her first jobs when she was nineteen. "He would
corner you in the stockroom . . . and expel gas, or he would
say little remarks or he would try to rub up against you. . . . I
was a virgin. I had no experience." She recalled him as being
six feet, five inches tall, frightening and "overwhelming."
She did the right thing and reported him, but she was the
one who got fired.

She had another bizarre experience when she struck out
on her own and moved into a girlfriend's house. She supported herself by working as a salesgirl in a department store.
But her friend unexpectedly got married, and Maria ended
up living not, as she had expected, with a girlfriend but with
a newlywed couple. The situation became stranger when the
husband's brother moved in also, and Maria was expected
to share a bedroom with him. Uncomfortable with those
arrangements, she moved back home.

At nineteen, Maria had sex for the first time, with an
older man who was actually a friend of her parents. Afraid
of their disapproval, fearful and guilty about sex, she chose
a man with whom she felt comfortable. Bob, thirty-three,
was going through a divorce and had a son who played ball
with one of her brothers. She felt she knew him; sex with
him would be safe emotionally because he was an old friend,
and because he had had a vasectomy, it carried no risk of
pregnancy.

Although she meant for her initiation into sex with Bob
to be relaxed, it turned into every Catholic girl's nightmare.
Only the presence of a neighborhood priest could have made
it worse. Maria left her car parked illegally near Bob's house,
and when Youngstown police broadcast they were going to
tow a car with her license plate number, her parents heard
it over their shortwave radio. They quickly figured out she
was spending the night at Bob's and showed up on the door-
step. "I was nineteen and he was thirty-three. . . . The only
reason I had sex was because I wanted to know what everybody else was talking about—and I hated it.

"I was afraid of my parents. I just knew that I wasn't

supposed to do it, and I was afraid that they'd find out and I was right. The very first time, they did find out."

Her father promptly had a "heart attack" and had to be taken to the hospital. Her mother called her "slut" and "whore." Her father's attack turned out to be irregular heartbeats, but he stopped talking to Maria for seven months. So her punishment for being sexual was meted out: She was annihilated. Her key to the house was symbolically taken back; she ceased to exist for her family.

Since sex for Maria was colored by fear and guilt and—now that she had been caught—by punishment, she had to do penance for her act with Bob. She had to suffer; sex came to represent not pleasure but suffering.

Her next sexual experience—the final one before she met her future husband, Jesse Califano—was a date with a "gorgeous guy" who took her to a secluded spot and tried to rape her. He only gave up when a truck parked nearby and he was frightened off by the fact of a potential witness. But like so many sexual-assault victims, Maria felt responsible. "I never told anybody about it until I told Phil."

When Maria was twenty, her brother, who worked in a gas station, introduced her to Jesse, twenty-three, just discharged from the Army and working for a company that rustproofed cars. The first time they met, Jesse immediately invaded Maria's privacy and established the parameters of their future relationship. "I had a T-shirt on. I don't even know what it said on it and he went, 'What does this say?' and he drug his finger across my chest."

She told him to keep his hands off her, but of course, he didn't. Maria didn't think Jesse was very nice, but she did find him "gorgeous." Maria likes good-looking men: "Pretty boys are easy on my eyes."

When Maria and Jesse slept together four months after they met, it was the first time she had ever enjoyed sex. "We had a few drinks and we smoked a joint and I was totally relaxed and I think that's why it was different."

With Jesse, she had fewer inhibitions and felt comfortable. But Maria never really overcame her repressive upbringing; she was married two months before she had enough nerve to see a gynecologist. "I was just afraid to go . . . and have an internal examination.

"I was naive as far as sex and birth control and everything. . . . I had never had sex explained to me. . . . I found out how babies were made in fourth grade in the girls' bathroom. . . . When I was growing up, I had a little Italian grandmother from the old country telling me, 'You crossa you legs and you tell 'em no touchin' my place.' " Maria picked up her mother's attitude toward sex, which was "she really didn't enjoy it a whole lot and . . . she thought it was because of *her* mother."

She married Jesse even though she knew he wasn't the knight in shining armor for whom she had been waiting. He was unpolished, rough, unschooled in the small niceties Maria's romantic fantasies led her to feel she deserved. But the sexual attraction was there; and it was time she got married.

She had just turned twenty-two when they married in August 1979, but her romantic fantasies were already dead. When Jesse told her to quit her job to be a full-time homemaker, she put up little resistance.

Jesse drank a lot while they were dating, but it wasn't until they lived together that Maria understood the extent of his addiction. He was an alcoholic and the marriage turned into a nightmare. When he was drunk, he abused Maria emotionally and physically. He would erupt into anger and destroy her most valued possessions. "He knew how important [something] was because my grandmother gave it to me, and he'd break it right in front of me to cause me to fight back with him. . . . I'd clean up whatever he destroyed and the next day he wouldn't believe me." He had blackouts and never remembered the violence.

He also pulled her hair, pushed her around, and intimidated her. One day, in a move eerily similar to Phil's murder of Tina, Jesse threatened Maria with a loaded gun. "He pointed it at my head and didn't remember. . . . He was in a blackout. I'm lucky my brother Jimmy was there because Jimmy talked it out of his hands."

Finally, Maria left Jesse. Once again, her family came through—but for Jesse, not for her. "My family's so crazy, my mother told him where I was at." Maria and Jesse reconciled, and for the next few years the relationship depended on how much Jesse drank. If he wasn't drunk, "he was the best person that you could ever want around you." But drunk, he became an abusive monster.

Things got worse when he was laid off from his job as a lineman in the paint department at General Motors. Maria got a part-time job teaching preschool; before July 1979, Ohio preschool teachers were not required to be college graduates or state certified. Although she was bringing in some money, Jesse didn't like it. He wanted to be the "man" of the family. Although he initially received 95 percent of his pay after his layoff, that was cut and Jesse was bored and rapidly becoming broke. He also had too much time for drinking. So he took a night job cleaning the offices of the local newspaper.

It was snowing on December 12, 1982, when Jesse went out to a meeting for his new night job. He told Maria to stay home, but uncharacteristically, she didn't listen and went out with friends instead. She still feels guilty she wasn't home when it happened. When she returned at about midnight, the phone was ringing. It was the Youngstown police telling her Jesse had been in an accident and was in a coma. No one knew if he'd slipped and fallen on ice or if he'd been mugged and hit over the head. At the age of twenty-five, after being married to a difficult, possessive, alcoholic man who abused her, Maria was left with a man *she* controlled, whose life was in her hands. Doctors told her Jesse would always be in "a vegetative state." Although he eventually returned to consciousness, he was never again recognizable as Jesse Califano.

Maria panicked; she had never had to make decisions before: "When I was younger, my father told me what to do. Then my mother told me what to do. Then when I was

married, my husband told me what to do." After Jesse's
head injury, she was on her own, burdened with total responsibility for another human being. For a while he was in
and out of various hospitals. Then in March 1983, Maria
checked Jesse into a Pittsburgh institution that specialized
in head injuries.

"He was more or less a vegetable. I planned to leave
him here and come on weekends." Maria was still living in
Youngstown, some ninety-five miles away, but eventually
moved to Pittsburgh so she could visit Jesse daily.

He remained in his own world, totally dependent on
others. "He can't talk because his brain won't let him." He
was left without the use of the right side of his body and
with the left side slightly spastic.

Maria grew increasingly uncomfortable with Jesse's
being in an institution. She began to see him as a victim, as
helpless. "Someone who is ill and left in the hands of doctors
and nurses and administrators is really like a kind of prisoner." She decided to take him home and hire private nurses
with the money she was collecting from the Ohio Bureau of
Worker's Compensation.

In part, Maria's empathy for prisoners was the result
of her recent involvement with an inmate. His name was
Phil Sylvester, and five years earlier he had murdered his
girlfriend.

MARIA AND PHIL

While Jesse was in the institution, Maria had become close
with a nurse, Lucy, who wanted Maria to meet her husband,
imprisoned for burglary. Although Maria liked Lucy and
wanted to meet her husband, she was a little shocked: "I
had never known anyone incarcerated before." Up to that
point, her world did not include criminals, but she agreed
to go because she knew her friend was anxious to have someone on the outside meet the man she loved.

On their way to the prison, an additional burden was

put on Maria when Lucy asked her to visit with another
inmate, a friend of her husband's who never received visitors
of his own. "My friend asked me to call out another gentle-
man. . . . I was scared. I never knew anybody in prison before. I guess maybe I grew up sheltered. I was afraid; I didn't
know what it would be like. I imagined the typical inmates
you see on television and the movies. But that wasn't what
I found."

On August 16, 1983, Maria Califano found herself ner-
vously approaching the State Correctional Institute of Pittsburgh. "I was really apprehensive. My knees knocked, and
when I went to sign in, my handwriting was shaking. When
they finally let us in, they have these doors that slam shut
and that's a terrible feeling."

In the visitors' room, a tall, good-looking man with dark
hair waited. "He walked up to me and I was just like amazed.
There was this normal-looking person standing in front of
me. He could have been my next-door neighbor. The man
I met was nothing like what I imagined." Maria returned
weekly to visit, and although she soon found out Phil was
serving a life sentence for murder, she fell in love with
him.

Phil was no longer the same arrogant young man who
had killed his girlfriend. He had been doing hard time in a
state correctional facility for five years. He had seen and
done and heard things he didn't want to think about.

Meeting Maria was a boost for Phil; she was attractive,
sexy, and willing to spend hours talking to him. For her, that
first meeting was merely pleasant: Maria and Phil talked
about their families for the entire three-hour visit. "It was
kind of uneventful. No, I didn't think anything of his looks
then. Now, of course, he's gorgeous. But at that point, he
was a nice-looking person. I just saw a nice guy. We talked
about my husband, his parents, his sisters and brothers."

Though she never intended to go back a second time—
she had done her good deed and visited a lonely inmate—
at some point she decided to visit again. "I had met a person
--**- looked like he could be my next-door neighbor. He was

intelligent; he came from a good family. I decided to go ahead and go back. You see, I didn't plan on staying in Pittsburgh that long because I was still living in the pipe dream that my husband was going to get up and walk and talk and everything."

Her decision to see Phil again was motivated solely by the desire to "do something nice for someone else." Maria admits, though, that if Phil were "ugly, I wouldn't have gone back. He asked me to visit and I continued each week to meet a sensitive, kind person. . . . I know it's hard to believe."

Phil was very interested. Many men in prison have women on the outside, and he wanted to be one of them. Maria was attractive with long black hair, smooth, clear skin, and a sensuous face and figure. She was warm, a good talker and listener.

It was not until their second visit that Phil told Maria why he was doing time. She accepted his version of the murder and believed that it was an accident. She was able to separate the crime from the man. "I initially wanted to do something nice for someone who needed it; [then] I was compelled to go back. . . . I needed to be stimulated intellectually. I guess because every day, all day, it was the same thing—medical, medical, medical—because of my husband."

She visited Phil once a week, the maximum allowed; they wrote and he called her—collect. Inmates can only call the outside world collect. Four months after they met, Phil told Maria he loved her. "Phil said, 'Since I've been in prison, these guys in here have tried to fix me up with everyone. But it's you I want. I want you in my life.'

"I panicked. It scared me; it wasn't what I had been looking for. I was looking for a friendship. At that time I still was in a dream world that everything would be okay with Jesse." But Phil began to become more and more important, his letters and phone calls the high points of her day. Eventually, Maria acknowledged that she was in love with him.

So many romantic, passionate letters went back and forth that Maria now has four shoeboxes full. Some were explicitly sexual—"I did get some smut letters, too."

Sex, however, was secondary. "There was so much love and so much romance and so much honesty and respect and truth." At her first meeting, while there was no love at first sight, there was a flicker of feeling—a feeling Maria had not had in a long time, perhaps a feeling she had never had. Someone was willing to listen to her, to talk to her. "I was attracted to him both with my mind and with my body. We had morals and ideals that were the same. I enjoyed his company."

She denied his crime, separating the Phil she was falling in love with from the Phil who had killed a woman. "I believe what he told me, [that] he did not know the gun was loaded. I believe him because he's been honest with me all along. I know what he's done wrong and I know what he's done right. And I love him regardless."

According to Maria, marks on Tina's neck indicating she was strangled before she was shot were made by her brother, not by Phil. "Her brother found out that she was prostituting herself out and that she was involved in drugs, and he smacked her around and choked her that morning." But Maria knows Phil actually did the killing. "He admits pointing the gun and pulling the trigger. But he says he did not know the gun was loaded and he did not mean to kill the woman. . . . He told me they used to have fistfights. They were arguing, I guess, and he did it more or less to scare her."

Phil and Tina, about to end their relationship, "had started becoming abusive to each other," and Phil had a gun in his possession. To Maria—whose husband, Jesse, had been abusive and who had once held a gun to her head—pointing a gun at someone to "scare" them is very much within the parameters of reality. One of her brothers has owned a gun; guns are an accepted part of her life. "I think all men go through this gun fascination."

But Maria believes murder is wrong, and according to

her, so does Phil. "Phil has a lot of remorse for what he did. He said it's something he'll live with every day for the rest of his life—that he can't begin to explain to me what it feels like to take another person's life, but it doesn't feel very good.

"It bothers me that he did something like this. I hope that what he's told me is the truth, and I do believe him." Maria said she believes Phil, then said that she *hopes* he's telling the truth. She has made the leap of faith; she is willing to believe his story because she is in love with him.

WOMEN WHO LOVE MEN WHO KILL

Maria's story is not unique. Unbelievable as it may seem, there is a population of women who are deeply drawn to men who have murdered. They meet the men while working in prisons as nurses, teachers, social workers, or volunteers. Others become pen pals with murderers. Some, who are infatuated, write fan/love letters to celebrity killers such as "Preppie Murderer" Robert Chambers or serial killers such as David Berkowitz, known as Son of Sam. A fellow inmate of Berkowitz's said that even today, more than a decade after his bizarre serial killings in New York City, he still receives letters from women who want to meet him. These women want to meet these killers because they are looking for love; some end up marrying these men.

"The women have reached the point in life where the magic words are 'one last chance.' . . . Most are unhappy, frustrated, and dissatisfied. They have low self-image and want to attach themselves to figures they think are power-ful," said psychiatrist David Abrahamsen, M.D., author of many books including *Confessions of Son of Sam* and the expert whose testimony convinced the court that Berkowitz was competent to stand trial.

In America—where single men and women are lonely and it's difficult to meet someone to love and relate to— killers seem to have no trouble finding girlfriends and wives.

Suspected murderers, indicted murderers, convicted murderers, even serial killers who confess to the most heinous crimes, are all able to find love. Once inside prison, a murderer, although usually serving a life sentence, often becomes a magnet for women.

In Holdrege, Nebraska, Police Chief Ken Jackson said it's a common phenomenon. He recalled a Lincoln man who shot his wife eight times; she died on the spot. "The first week he was in jail, seven women came to visit him." These women, who were previously unacquainted with the murderer, appeared to "fall madly in love through the little glass window" in the visiting room.

Robert Chambers was so popular with young women during his trial that his groupies were dubbed the Bobbettes by the *New York Post.* "They hung all over him, fawned all over him," said an observer.

Before the trial began, but after jury selection, Chambers was the centerpiece of a sensational home video made by some of his friends. In the video, he is seen twisting the neck of a doll—who many believe represents his victim, Jennifer Levin—and prancing around, fully dressed, with a number of partially clad, suggestively dancing, young women.

The prisons are full of killers who have women on the outside, waiting, hoping, assaulting the legal system relentlessly, determinedly, so their men will get a parole, a pardon, a commutation, a new trial.

THE WOMEN

These women are of all types. Like Maria, some are housewives married to other men. Others are professionals—teachers, nurses, reporters, social workers. Even women lawyers and judges are not immune to this fascination.

Some women, in pink-collar jobs, work in factories, offices, and service industries as waitresses, house cleaners, cooks, nurses' aides, secretaries. Many of the women have children; others are childless. They are all ages, but the majority seem to be in their thirties and forties.

They may be well educated with bachelor's degrees, even some Ph.D.'s and law degrees. Some have only high school diplomas while others never got past the sixth grade.

Other than their romantic entanglements with murderers, these women have no involvement with the criminal world. Like Maria, most of these women never visited a prison before they met their men. Nor have they themselves committed any crimes. They consider themselves moral, upright, caring, right-thinking Americans. They are good women—who developed from the good girls they were as children. They generally don't use illegal drugs; not many drink. They are frequently religious. They believe in family, honor, tradition, and the American flag.

These women are the well-groomed, neatly dressed members of the PTA, the church group, or the garden club. They are the women we see in the supermarket, behind desks, in subways and on buses, taking their children to the park, visiting their elderly parents. *They look normal; they look just like ordinary people.* They never caused much trouble as teenagers; as adults they have been law-abiding citizens. They have not indulged in deviant behavior; they have not been arrested.

But they stray from the norm in one enormous way. Their emotions and needs and deepest desires have led them to form passionate, romantic alliances with men who have committed murder—the outcasts of the same society they symbolize.

These women are acting out their deepest fantasies. They find love, romance, passion, and commitment where society says they shouldn't: with killers, the masters of death, the men who take the lives of others, men who have committed crimes ranging from a brutal single murder to a hideous series of killings.

These women find men who kill glamorous, romantic, sexual, and lovable. The murders don't put the women off; they are not frightened by the idea of killing. While the rest of us might find these men frightening or repulsive, to their women, they are desirable. These women want to meet them, talk to them, love them, be with them.

While the world shuddered at the unspeakable horror of serial killer Ted Bundy, scores of women found him appealing enough to write to him. Dozens visited him in prison, and during his last trial, the courtroom was crowded with Ted groupies. Carole Ann Boone found him so fascinating and appealing that she married him near the end of his trial and later had his child.

Serial killers, the acknowledged masters of death, are enormously attractive to women. "Hillside Stranglers" Kenneth Bianchi and Angelo Buono killed more than a dozen women in California after raping, sodomizing, and torturing them. Bianchi pleaded guilty in 1979, and although he had to wait ten years, he is finally a groom. A Louisiana woman fell in love with him after a three-year courtship through the mail, and they married in September 1989, the day after they first met face to face.

Preppie Murderer Robert Chambers is still so appealing that he has not been without a girlfriend since his 1986 homicide, and after he was imprisoned in 1988, prison guards reported that a "bevy of beauties" visited him regularly. According to the district attorney who prosecuted Chambers, a manslaughter conviction was the only one possible because of the jury's confusion over Chambers's culpability in Jennifer Levin's death. Their confusion was further complicated by one juror, Elizabeth Bauch, who became "besotted with Chambers" during the trial. "She fell in love with him," said Linda Fairstein, assistant district attorney in Manhattan. "For nine days [while the jury was sequestered] she refused to discuss the evidence." (Bauch denies Fairstein's allegation.)

Elizabeth Bauch is not the only woman juror who ever fell in love with a murder defendant. In California in 1987 a man was convicted of kidnapping, rape, and murder but was not sentenced to death because one juror, Rochelle, was convinced "it was an accident." Sentenced to life without parole, this man received a visitor shortly after his conviction: Rochelle. Today they are husband and wife, and she is working hard to get him a new trial.

There are other cases as shocking:

- The former justice of the peace in a Western state who is married to a convicted killer.
- The Southern lawyer who, sent to represent a man accused of murder, helped him escape. After they were caught, she was disbarred and sent to prison herself. He has since married another woman and has fathered a child.
- The New York City fashion designer who gave up custody of her own daughter to "mother" the children of the suspected killer with whom she fell in love.

Although these women are diverse in their lifestyles and backgrounds, they are all prisoners of love in almost the same way their men are prisoners of various correctional systems. These women can't help themselves. They *must* be in these relationships in order to fulfill their very deepest needs, their most complex emotional dependencies, their ultimate fantasies. They are compelled to dance with the masters of death: These relationships are their lives. They are women obsessed.

THE MEN

They have killed either a family member—wife, girlfriend, relative—or murdered an outsider—a bank guard, a police officer, a random victim.

The men are diverse racially and ethnically but appear to have more similarities than their women on the outside. Few of them received much education before they committed murder, and many had miserable childhoods. The majority were substance abusers. The murders they committed often occurred while they were under the influence—and while they were still relatively young men. (Except for serial killers, who appear to be older than other murderers.)

Many of these men, while in prison, have tried to improve themselves. They attended classes after they were behind steel and concrete, acquiring high school, college, and even graduate degrees. Many of the lifers have become jailhouse lawyers, spending every waking moment studying law books, convinced they will never get out unless they fight their cases themselves. Some have found new careers behind bars because they were forced to find something with which to occupy themselves in the dead world of prison.

The men are often handsome and well built, like Robert Chambers or Ted Bundy. They are usually intense and charismatic, such as Jack Henry Abbott, a lifer who was released after pressure from various intellectuals who admired his book *In the Belly of the Beast*. He killed a man two months later and is serving a life sentence in New York State; he, too, has a woman on the outside.

Occasionally, these men appear more ordinary, like Kevin, who was convicted in 1985 of rape and murder. His devoted girlfriend, Lori, visits him once a week for six hours and writes and calls him daily. Kevin, a quiet man with nothing of the charismatic charmer about him, is a rarity among murderers who attract women on the outside.

These killers are strivers, not content to sit behind the walls and do nothing. In addition to seeking education and new careers, they seek love relationships because they know, after they've been in prison a short time, that having a woman on the outside is a big plus. She is a liaison with the world, a devoted advocate. Also, for a murderer trying to get paroled, having a stable relationship creates a positive impression on the parole board. A woman on the outside can often help get an inmate out—and when you're in prison, getting out is all that counts.

BUT IS IT LOVE?

These women are compelled to do what the majority of us would find dangerous and threatening. They go into prisons. They receive collect phone calls from murderers. They write to killers. They long for the day when their murderer/lover will be released from prison so they can be together. Even though their men have been convicted of violent murders, women on the outside are not afraid of sharing a home, a bed, a life, with them. They can't wait until their men are released so they can all—woman, children, murderer—live together in one big, happy family.

These women have found love in the least likely place, where society tells them it's forbidden, in the hostile environment of courtrooms and prisons. They have found passion in uncomfortable public prison visiting rooms watched over by unfriendly guards. Some dress in special ways—such as skirts without underpants—so they can have intercourse behind vending machines, in corners, on chairs, on benches; with their children watching; standing up, sitting down; in closets; in private rooms with entrée obtained by bribing guards—rarely in a bed. They have found commitment in relationships with men who are con artists, who will promise anything to get an extra pack of cigarettes. They enjoy the security of marriage with men who have broken the most sacred laws of humanity by killing.

But to these women, the love, passion, and commitment are more real and meaningful than if found in ordinary ways, with average men. Their relationships are the most important things in their lives. For women in love with murderers, the relationships are their reasons for being.

Most average wives and girlfriends don't give to a relationship the time and energy these women do. If they have telephone answering machines, the messages all say, "Yes, operator, I accept collect calls," so they never miss a message from their lovers in prison. These women are obsessed, addicted; their men are central to their lives. They build their work and family life around the men. They organize their weeks so they can make time-consuming prison visits. They spend a large part of their time talking about their men, fantasizing about the day they'll get out and they can finally be together.

But is it love or obsession? Is it healthy or unhealthy? Are these "good girls" loving "bad boys" for the wrong reasons? Do they get turned on sexually by the idea their men have killed? Is there prestige and excitement in loving the baddest of the bad guys? What is the particular and peculiar chemistry involved in an attraction to a killer? Are these women strange, deviant? Or are they normal, regular people who happened to fall into bizarre relationships? Are they society's most passionate women, refusing to brook any obstacle in the way of their love? Why *do* they fall in love with men who have killed?

MARIA'S STORY

When Maria fell in love with Phil, she was already in a prison of sorts herself, responsible twenty-four hours a day for a totally helpless husband. "The reason I'm not in love with my husband is because it's changed. He is now my child; I have motherly feelings for him because he does not walk or talk."

Jesse had abused her emotionally and physically for the duration of their marriage before his accident. But Maria does not focus on his cruelty; she just talks about what is now—his dependent state. She is exacting some kind of revenge for Jesse's cruel treatment of her. A visit to Maria's house reveals it is divided into "his," and "hers." Maria's larger part of the house is light, airy, roomy, and comfortable, decorated with beautiful plants, comfortable couches and chairs, and aesthetically pleasing colors. Jesse's bedroom and sitting room, on the other hand, are small, crowded, and infinitely darker. He is definitely under her control.

Phil, too, is a controllable relationship. He can't beat Maria, abuse her—or even leave his socks lying on the living-room floor. He can't place demands on her—for sex, for a good meal, for anything. For Maria, both Jesse and Phil are safe relationships. And while she says she longs for Phil's release, since Pennsylvania gives no paroles on life sentences, it's unlikely he will ever get out.

The relationship with Phil is also safe because no sex is involved. Maria, making it clear that she is not one of *those* women who have sex in the visiting room, treasures the nonsexual aspects of her relationship with Phil. "You don't have the sexual pressures of the outside world; you have each other. You do a lot of talking. You get involved emotionally."

After a lifetime of being sexually mauled by men, Maria is not interested in sex. "He [Phil] makes me very happy. . . . I have a husband who can't function and I have a boyfriend who can't function, but I'm happy. The love I get from Jesse and the love I get from Phil—I'm frustrated sexually, but I am content."

For Maria, a relationship without sexual pressures is highly desirable because her sexual past was a nightmare, ranging from a harassing boss to date rape, from a grandmother who said boys shouldn't be "touchin' her place" to a father who had a "heart attack" the night she lost her virginity. It's easier for Maria to live without sex.

It is likely that most women who love killers sentenced to life terms will never have normal sex with them. Yet, like Maria, the women interviewed for this book said they are willing to live lives of potential permanent sexual abstinence. Maria, like other women in her situation, "lives in a different reality and is caught up in a different emotional system" where a life of sexual abstinence is possible, according to clinical psychologist Stuart Fischoff, Ph.D. "These women are hooked in a way we can't comprehend."

Maria gets quite a bit from her relationship with Phil, in addition to freedom from sexual pressure. First, she feels powerful; she is in charge—she can write if she wants, visit when she feels like it, and accept his collect phone calls if she chooses. She has said her father, mother, and husband always told her what to do. But with Phil, she calls the shots.

During her childhood, Maria protected and mothered her five younger brothers. Once again, she's a protector: Both Phil and Jesse are dependent on her. She gains value and self-esteem in that role. It also fits in with her tendency to infantilize men. She calls Phil "boyfriend of mine" and "my young boy." She also has a cat named Boyfriend and usually refers to handsome men as "pretty boys."

On the other hand, she is aware that a man convicted of murder, an inmate in a tough prison, is not a baby. "They're not called cons because they're nice, sweet, innocent little boys. They are manipulators." Phil is different and Maria appreciates that he's never used her. But the district attorney who prosecuted Phil more than a decade ago said he was "a manipulator who had gotten [Tina] to stay with him" through control and trickery.

Maria has emotional and psychological needs that are being met for the first time in her life. Phil treats her as if she is important, and he is an excellent listener because, in essence, he is a captive audience. "I need to be stimulated. . . . This is an intellectual relationship. . . . I want to be appreciated for something other than sex."

Used to men pawing at her—Jesse "drug his finger across my chest" the night they met—Maria is totally dependent on the communicative relationship she has with Phil. Maria needed to be valued as a person, rather than a sex object.

According to psychiatrist Neil S. Kaye, M.D., this is the first time a man has "stuck up for Maria." Prison is a place where inmates "will go to the mat to defend their women; they will do anything to defend her honor, even hole time." (The hole is solitary confinement.) Maria needed a relationship that would supply her with this loyalty and with the attention, interaction, and nonsexual warmth that she craved. Phil is totally there for her, and she feels enriched by this intimacy. As we will see with other women who love murderers, Maria's father was somewhat cold, removed, and authoritarian. She said she was "scared to death" to go home when her grades weren't up to par or when she had committed some infraction of the house rules. Her first experience with sex is more memorable for her father's incredibly cruel behavior than for anything else. (When he had his "heart attack," he refused to allow Maria to go to the hospital with him. He did, however, allow her lover to accompany him.)

Maria's parents either never understood the severity of the abuse she suffered at Jesse's hands, or never cared. Remember, when Jesse was drying out and Maria had left him, her mother revealed her whereabouts, and the result was that Maria went back to Jesse. Now, in Phil, Maria has someone to give her advice. She credits Phil with her decision to remove Jesse from the nursing home. "If it wasn't for the strength and the courage he gave me, I don't believe I could have fought for my husband the way I did. Phil said, 'Maria, Jesse is in prison just like I am.' "

Initially she felt guilty about loving Phil, but she no longer does. "In the beginning I held myself back . . . but I give Jesse the best life possible. People like him are rotting away in nursing homes; he has a normal life now." Since Maria lives on the money she receives for Jesse from the Ohio Bureau of Worker's Compensation, it is unclear how much of her caring for Jesse at home is sacrifice and how much is her desire to have him under her thumb, to punish him for what he did to her.

BUT WHY A MURDERER?

Passionate love can be healthy or unhealthy. The lover may grow and become a better person, or she may become subjugated to her beloved, willing to become a slave to negative forces in exchange for being loved. Being central to another person is a major part of what love is about. Maria is now central to both Jesse—in his weakened, dependent state—and to Phil, in his imprisoned state.

As lovers do, Maria identifies with Phil's values, persona, and personal history. Some of these things she sees as crucial, while others she disavows and plays down. Maria emphasizes Phil's morals, which she says are the same as hers, and his "good" values—as when he sends cards and letters to Jesse and uses Jesse's therapy techniques on an inmate who is similarly handicapped.

But like the other women in this book who love killers, Maria denies Phil's responsibility for the murder he committed. When he says he didn't know the gun was loaded, she believes him. She is not at all afraid of being hurt by Phil. "I know him. He's a good, caring, loving man, and he has good morals and good ideals."

"It wasn't an accident why Maria chose this particular man," said psychoanalyst Carl Rotenberg, M.D., who believes that to be involved in a loving way with someone who has murdered, one must identify to a certain extent with that act and with the motivation for that act. Phil's murder "was a killing of a partner, and I think Maria had her own issues about wanting her partner to die," said Rotenberg. Phil killed someone who was difficult to live with, who rejected him and did not return his love. These are emotions and experiences Maria had during her early relationship with Jesse. It's likely that during her marriage, Maria had murderous feelings toward Jesse. Phil's murder of Tina is, symbolically, Maria's murder of Jesse. (But since Maria herself almost died at Jesse's hands when he held a loaded gun to her head, she very likely also identifies with Phil's victim.)

That Phil has killed is central to Maria's love for him. Even while she denies his culpability, it is his ability to murder that attracts her. His murder of Tina means he *acted* on his rage, however unsuitably. Maria could never act on her rage, cultivating a good-girl image, agreeing to everything imposed on her. Remember: "My father told me what to do. Then my mother told me what to do. Then my husband told me what to do."

So Phil's murder is also Maria's murder. She said they share everything: morals, values, ideals. They also share this killing. It finally brings closure to the unresolved rage she felt during her life toward her family for turning her, too young, into a "second mother," toward her father for being unavailable and authoritarian, toward men for seeing her only as a sex object, toward her mother for not adequately protecting her from the men who hurt her, and finally, toward her husband for his drinking and abusive behavior.

Loving Phil has also given Maria a sense of power. In its broadest perspective, murder means exercising control over life and death. This power is incredibly attractive to others; weak individuals feel they can draw from it, become powerful themselves. So Maria identifies with Phil's power—he had actually done what she had wanted to do herself.

Phil crossed the line between being enraged enough to want to kill—and killing. It was not an accident that Maria fell in love with him. The fact that he listened to her and was concerned about her—any inmate would have served that need. But only someone who took another life could fill her deep need to be enmeshed in that kind of—what she perceives to be—strength. A powerless woman living a life of emptiness and constriction, Maria has drawn energy and vigor from her killer/lover.

Because he's incarcerated and she is a free agent, Maria has a large amount of control over this relationship. If Phil is powerful because he has taken a life, how powerful then is Maria? "It's hard to come up with anything more powerful than to be in control of someone powerful enough to take a life," said Dr. Kaye. "This raises self-esteem and self-image considerably." Maria is in the driver's seat and her passenger is a murderer; for the first time in her life, Maria is an important person.

DENIAL

In order to allow oneself to love a killer, a certain amount of denial has to take place. Women who love men who have murdered talk easily about their battles to free their lovers, and they can discuss their romances—how they met, how love flourished in the ugly prison atmosphere. They can explain how the prison system is slowly eroding what's left of their lovers' spirits and how the system treats them as if the stigma of loving an inmate makes them into monsters, also.

But when it comes to the murder itself, an element of unreality creeps in. None will say her lover has the capacity to kill. Although the evidence is there, although the facts are known, not a single woman believes that her man *really* did it—even though he stands convicted. These women engage in denial and compartmentalization. They put the crime aside when thinking about the men they love. They have excuses, like Maria's, that Phil didn't know the gun was loaded.

In the following chapters, we will meet other women whose lives are devoted to the murderers they love, each woman spinning dizzily in a dance with a master of death. The fact that her lover has killed is part of his importance and serves to meet her emotional and psychological needs. Because they are so dangerous and difficult, these relationships are extremely intense, burning with all the passion we have come to expect from romantic love as it is depicted in romance novels and soap operas.

Some of these women love men who are notorious. Others love murderers whose names have long since faded from the headlines. But all women who love killers share the same need to sacrifice themselves to a love that is so intense, it is potentially threatening. Like moths around a flame, even if they get burned, these women continue to hover around their lovers as long as they are wanted.

2

Murder and Marriage

"It was hardly romantic"

THE PHENOMENON

The phenomenon of women loving murderers challenges everything that is socially, morally, and ethically acceptable. It defies rational understanding and seems to be incomprehensible and unexplainable.

Many criminal-justice experts and mental-health specialists—generally male—tend to dismiss these women as suffering from a personality disorder. But these women are not freaks or fools. They are examples of what can happen in our brutal, patriarchal society in which women strive to keep up at least the appearance of social propriety by getting married—even if it's marriage to a murderer. These women should not be condemned, relegated to the outskirts of society, or written off. Nor should they be stigmatized and ostracized as they often are because of their relationships with killers.

They cross class, religion, and race lines. They work in

48

all sorts of jobs, have varying income levels, different educations. They might be categorized as "women who love too much," but as we'll see later, they absolutely don't love too much. They don't really love at all.

For some, it's the "good girl" looking for the "bad boy." She is afraid of being bored so chooses to be a gangster's "moll." She always feels special because he loves her, and *he* is a wild man, an outcast, deadly and dangerous. John Money, Ph.D., a pioneering sexuality researcher, has coined a term for being turned on by danger: *hybristophilia*. It's a paraphilia, or sexual perversion, in which arousal is dependent on being with a partner known to have committed a violent crime—such as murder. A woman with this perversion is sexually "turned on only by a partner who has a predatory history of outrages perpetrated on others," writes Money, in *Lovemaps*.

No murderer is too despicable; somewhere there is a woman who will love him. Even James Earl Ray, convicted killer of the Reverend Dr. Martin Luther King, Jr., managed to find a wife. In early 1978, Anna Sandhu, thirty-two, an artist for a television station doing a documentary on Ray, sat across from the notorious assassin studying the lines and angles and planes of his face. Using charcoals and pastels, she drew him over and over. An attractive blonde with a great figure, a talented artist, Anna began doing little favors for Ray. By the time she began visiting him regularly, the documentary was long finished. Anna was drawn in by Ray's cries for help and his refusal to admit his guilt. She checked facts, interviewed people, tried to help him prove he was innocent. She fell in love.

James Earl Ray and Anna Sandhu were married in October 1978 at Brushy Mountain Penitentiary in Tennessee where Ray was serving a ninety-nine-year term. She wore an off-white, pleated skirt and matching crocheted blouse. "I love him. I know we have a lot of adversity ahead of us, but we're ready to face it," Sandhu said in the *New York Times*. She had done the proposing; she had even torn her panty hose getting down on her knees. Anna was sure the

courts would set a release date for her husband—who she
believed had been framed—if he had a wife waiting for him.
After the brief ceremony, and a ten-minute honeymoon during which they were alone but under the scrutiny of four
guards, Anna went home—alone.

A reporter for a national newspaper, Joe Mullins,
couldn't believe how naive and innocent Anna was when he
met with her. In Tennessee to cover the wedding, he was
staying at the Holiday Inn. Anna came to his room for a
prearranged interview but refused to talk to Mullins unless
the door was kept open. He sat on the green-striped bed-
spread, but she sat primly in a straight-backed chair. Mullins
offered her $15,000 for an exclusive but she refused, saying
publicity would hurt her husband's chances for freedom.

During the couple's twelve-year marriage, they consummated their love at least once. "James had been attacked
in jail, and badly hurt, and was moved to a prison hospital.
I visited him there and we were able to make love. It was
wonderful—we were husband and wife at last," she told
reporter Mullins twelve years later in a 1990 interview. But
she described most of her prison visits as "heartrending. We
couldn't even touch or kiss. Two women attendants used to
subject me to humiliating searches making nasty comments."

The marriage was a disaster for Anna. Because people
knew who she was, she couldn't sell her art anywhere, was
accused of being a racist, and even received death threats.
By the end, she had gained more than sixty pounds and Ray
was taunting her about her weight. Eventually Anna stopped
visiting. "I think his enthusiasm cooled when he realized he
was not going to get out of prison—with or without a wife,"
she told Mullins. In March 1990, *Ray* filed for divorce.

Although it is stated in our moral code that one must
not kill, we often settle our differences violently. "Our big-
gest failure in the socialization of the human animal has been
the prevalence of murder. . . . We have never decided to

abolish homicide; we merely regulate it," writes Dr. Emanuel Tanay in *The Murderers*.

Both individual and serial killings are increasing, and in 1992, according to FBI supervisory special agent William Hagmaier III, we can expect the number of murders around the country to equal the population of a small city—at least 22,000. The murderers who are caught, convicted, and imprisoned often attract women to them, with the result that a small but very interesting subculture of couples, composed of murderers and free women, is growing every day.

Women's romantic relationships with murderers are confusing to police, prosecutors, and prison officials although they are quite aware of the existence of these relationships. Officials are often upset about a convicted murderer's having a love affair with a free woman. Imagine spending five years tracking down the Hillside Stranglers and another two years testifying during their trials—only to find out that these men are getting married!

Granted, a woman who marries a serial killer is different from a woman who marries a man who has killed once. But how different? Women who love killers have fallen in love with the most spectacularly antisocial portion of our society. They rain their kisses on mouths that have cursed as they pulled the trigger, they hold hands that have strangled, they caress arms that have wielded weapons of death. No matter whether the man has killed once, or ten times, he has taken human life. He has done the unthinkable. He is a pariah forever, doomed to dwell on the fringes of society wherever society knows the truth about him. Once a community finds out a convicted murderer is in its midst—even one who's paroled or pardoned—residents may chase the man out of the town or city. Their instincts are sometimes correct.

One such pariah was Arthur J. Shawcross, who, paroled from prison in 1987 after serving fifteen years of a twenty-five-year sentence for manslaughter, was hounded out of two communities. Shawcross, convicted in 1972 of sexually molesting and strangling an eight-year-old girl in his hometown of Watertown, New York, and believed to be responsible for killing a ten-year-old boy, tried living in Binghamton, New York, after his parole.

Driven out of Binghamton by outraged citizens, Shawcross then moved to Delhi, a small nearby town. There, inhabitants were again angry and fearful, and police officials told Shawcross they were watching him closely. Four weeks later, he moved to Rochester, New York.

Unfortunately, the people, press, and police of Rochester were not so vigilant. Shawcross settled down, waited a few months, and then began killing. In January 1990, he was arrested for strangling at least eleven women. After a ten-week trial, Shawcross was found guilty and convicted of murder in December 1990.

Shawcross has found a woman to love him—actually, two women. He has a wife, his fourth, Rosemary, whom he met while he was in prison; they were pen pals. When he was paroled, they married. After they moved to Rochester, he also began seeing another woman, Clara. According to the Monroe County district attorney, Howard R. Relin, it is likely that Clara also knew of Shawcross's murderous past. She may even have suspected that he was busy killing during his months in Rochester. Clara "was very helpful with the investigation," said Rochester police spokesman Sgt. Ronald Marchetti. Since Shawcross's arrest on charges of strangling the eleven women, both his wife and his girlfriend have continued to visit him in prison, said the district attorney.

MURDERERS

Convicted murderers, the love objects of the women described in this book, have been found guilty of taking at least one life. Although society scorns these killers, a totally different view is expressed by the women who love them: Most believe their men to be innocent—or if not totally innocent, then not completely responsible either. Told by their men that either they did not commit murder—or did, under extenuating circumstances—their women believe them. Not one woman interviewed for this book said that her husband or boyfriend had murdered. They spoke of accidental killings, self-defense, manslaughter, "an unfortunate accident."

Here's the tricky part. Even though these women deny their men have murdered, *underneath the denial, there is a place where each woman knows that her man is a killer.* She sees him imprisoned for murder; she closely reads every word of his trial transcript and every news clipping she can get her hands on. So she knows that he is a murderer. But what she subconsciously has knowledge of and what she's willing to admit are two different things.

So even though she denies that he's a murderer, he can, at the same time, appeal to her *as* a murderer. His bloodlust, his killing, is enormously sexual and erotic to her—at the same time she's telling the world that he's innocent.

In our culture, murderers have enormous allure. Here is Robin Morgan's description of the appeal of a terrorist (substitute *murderer*) in *The Demon Lover: On the Sexuality of Terrorism:* "His mystique is the latest version of the Demon Lover. He evokes pity because he lives in death. He emanates sexual power because he represents obliteration. He excites the thrill of fear. He is the essential challenge to tenderness. He is at once a hero of risk and antihero of mortality."

Murderers find love relationships with women no matter how, why, or whom they have killed. To cover the attraction they feel toward the men's violence, the women focus on their men's normalcy. These may be convicted murderers, but they eat, sleep, talk, walk, do all the things everyone else does. Since most people think they can look at a person and tell if he's a murderer, these women evaluate the men they love and say: "He could have been my next-door neighbor"—therefore he's not capable of murder.

CAREER CRIMINALS

Some men murder during the commission of another felony: They kill owners of businesses, clerks, or other employees, hapless customers, bystanders, passersby. They kill police officers who try to arrest them. Most career criminals take up crime as simply as other men take up any other work: It's there, and in the circles they travel, it's socially acceptable. Career criminals begin at an early age with petit larceny, auto thefts, small burglaries, and then work their way up to larger crimes such as armed robbery, assault, possibly rape and murder.

Career criminals spend a major portion of their lives in prison. Jack, fifty-seven, is serving a life sentence in Colorado for a murder he says he did not commit. In 1983, he married a high school teacher ten years his junior, Annette, who is passionately in love with him. Asked how many burglaries he committed, in 1984 he told a reporter: "I couldn't even begin to count—maybe 350 to 500, something like that." Convicted of only a tiny percentage of these crimes, he's been in and out of jail since he was twelve. He served his first term in state prison in 1958. Now, three decades later, he is still in prison, but there is a likelihood he will be paroled in the near future.

He never said he robbed because he needed the money. He described his burglaries as an addiction. Even though he held down a regular job, he would pull burglaries on his lunch hour just for the thrill; for that reason, Jack is an anomaly. Most career criminals commit crimes in order to make money. His wife, Annette, explains why Jack robbed and killed: "He was a child in the Kentucky hills. His dad had black-lung disease and was an alcoholic. His mother was fourteen when she got married. I think there was no supervision. . . . They were so poor, there was no bathroom. . . . The first thing he can remember was stealing Christmas presents for his family when he was ten."

Jack, in an essay published in a Colorado newspaper, explained "career" criminals. None of the thousands of men he had seen "come and go into and out of jails" since his initial exposure in 1951 "liked" being imprisoned. "Why, then, the continued involvement with antisocial acts that can only lead to incarceration? Are we merely 'criminals'? I honestly don't know one single criminal. Not one. Some come close to fitting that classification, but none is firmly in that column. Are we just a bunch of 'sickies' who can't be helped? I'd tend to favor that analogy, for there is a sickness involved and we can't, under the present system of mishandling the problem, be helped. . . . Man is a victim of his own environment. When restriction, abuse, condemnation, isolation, and despair become a way of life, those enemies no longer frighten a person. They make him angry, and it's that anger that becomes the driving force in his life and dooms him to return to jail time after time."

Others tend to have a less sympathetic view of career criminals. "A man who kills a holdup victim is a psychopath, with little conscience, a macho kind of guy who likely beat up his girlfriends before," said Dr. Tanay. Women who love killers are usually involved with these sadistic, macho, career criminals, he believes. For the most part, my interviews bear him out. The majority of women in this book are in love with men who became involved in crime when they were very young and then evolved into murderers: They were and are "bad boys."

But there are many exceptions.

EMOTIONAL MURDERERS

Some of the women in this population are romantically involved with men who have killed out of passion, such as Phil in Chapter 1. So-called family or emotional killings are far greater in number than other murders because they include domestic murders. Men who kill women—girlfriends or wives—and other family members such as parents or children are categorized by police and psychiatrists as emotional killers, as opposed to those who murder as part of their crime careers. Generally, these men are seriously psychologically damaged and have great problems dealing with reality. They are less dangerous to the world at large than is the career criminal, but are far more dangerous to the people they "love."

"A person who has been involved in family conflict is usually . . . very passive and submissive and has had an explosive episode [during which he murdered]. He would have an underdeveloped conscience. . . . There would be a certain kind of woman who needs that kind of man," said Dr. Tanay.

Psychiatrist Park Elliot Dietz, M.D., Ph.D., agreed that murders within the family typically involve a person who is noncriminal but "disturbed in some way, including intoxicated, depressed, psychotic, under pressure, and unable to cope." These disturbed states don't last; at other times, a month, a week, even a day later, these people can be quite normal.

"Someone who ends up killing within the family is often either psychotic or has problems with dependency, loss, or separation," said forensic social worker Janet Warren, DSW. Very often, these family murders take place when a wife or girlfriend says she is leaving or wants to end the relationship. (Tina wanted to break up with Phil; he killed her.)

From 60 to 80 percent of all murders are these emotionally charged family killings, according to Dr. Tanay in *The Murderers:* "Homicide, so to speak, is most often an affair of the heart . . . a family affair because family members both love and hate one another, and the hate, if it becomes excessive, may explode in murder . . . there are those among us who are fury-driven to passions they cannot endure and who will lift the knife, the gun, the tormented hand . . ."

SERIAL KILLERS

A third category of murderers is comprised of serial killers and mass murderers: Ted Bundy, the Hillside Stranglers, Richard Ramirez, John Wayne Gacy. In the scores of books about them and their sensational crimes, they are described as pure evil, psychotic, criminally insane. Despite these labels, each of these men has had a woman at his side *after his conviction*, loving him, believing in him, willing and eager to marry him!

Veronica Lynn "VerLynn" Compton is in prison for life because her passion for Kenneth Bianchi, one of the two Hillside Stranglers, made her into a criminal herself. VerLynn started writing to Bianchi while he was in jail in L.A. An attractive model who had just won a contract to represent a company, it's not clear what prompted her to contact the notorious killer except, perhaps, his notoriety. Bianchi began romancing her, and they were soon seeing each other daily. She followed him to Bellingham, Washington, where he was about to stand trial for the murder of two coeds.

Sitting close together in the prison visiting room, the two hatched the plan that would lead to VerLynn's life sentence. I want to help you, VerLynn told Kenneth. If you want to help me, he said, kill someone. That will prove you're really willing to put yourself on the line. They decided she had to kill a woman using the Strangler style. It wouldn't be easy. There were insurmountable problems. She left the prison that day and drove away thinking how she could pull it off.

During their next visit, the couple tried to come up with a method for her to lure a woman into trusting her. They thought of all sorts of crazy plans, even one in which she would dress as a nun. Finally, Kenneth said to her, Just do it. Then after the body is discovered, I'll tell detectives that obviously I'm not the Hillside Strangler since the slayings are still going on.

VerLynn loved Bianchi so much she was willing to kill for him. But they had one logistical problem they couldn't solve: How could she anoint the victim's body with semen? She had to, in order to imitate the sexual abuse that always accompanied the Stranglers' torture-murders. Finally, they decided VerLynn would go to a sperm bank and obtain some semen.

Two nights later, VerLynn was set to try her first murder. She took a room at the Best Western Heritage Inn in Bellingham, then went to a bar near the motel and chatted with a woman who was sitting alone. VerLynn said she was staying nearby and would the woman like to come back to the room with her for a drink? The woman, a tall redhead, agreed. Once inside VerLynn's room, VerLynn leaped on her would-be victim, hands around her throat, squeezing tight. But the woman was sinewy and pushed her attacker off, escaping into the night.

Limping—she had lost her black high heel—sobbing, her neck raw and painful, the redhead walked to a pay phone and called the police. She told them a woman had tried to strangle her. They came to pick her up and get her statement; in the meantime, VerLynn fled back to California. It was obvious she didn't have what it takes to be a Hillside Strangler. She didn't contact Kenneth.

Bellingham detectives, working with the L.A. Sheriff's Department, identified VerLynn, piecing together the Bellingham woman's description and what they knew of the model's relationship with Bianchi. VerLynn was arrested, tried, and convicted and is now serving a life term in Bellingham for attempted murder. But VerLynn is still kicking. About two years ago, she and another women escaped from the Washington State penitentiary where they are housed. The escape was brief, though. They were quickly caught and returned to prison.

There is speculation among law enforcement agents that VerLynn's escape was an attempt to get free so she could contact her beloved Kenneth; she may have heard through the prison grapevine that he was planning to marry. But she never got to him, and in 1989, Bianchi married another woman.

MURDER CONVICTIONS

If convicted, a murderer is sentenced by the state in which he committed his crime to either life without parole, death, or a long prison term. For many women, the length of a murderer's term is intrinsically tied up with his appeal. She can become involved, certain he will remain in jail either for the rest of his life or for decades to come. Murderers are not quickly or easily released. Eighteen states have life without parole, and thirty-eight have the death penalty.

But on occasion, a murderer is convicted of a lesser charge because he is allowed to plea bargain. This happened in the Shawcross case. Although in 1972 he admitted to killing two children, he was never charged with murder. The *New York Times* of January 13, 1990, reported that Jefferson County district attorney Gary W. Miles said Shawcross was originally "spared a murder charge and a life term in exchange for telling authorities where he had hidden the body of a 10-year-old" boy. He was charged only in the killing of a girl, and for that crime, was convicted of manslaughter and sentenced to twenty-five years. Shawcross was released to kill again after serving only fifteen years for "good time."

In cases where the evidence is inconclusive and prosecutors feel they would have a tough time convincing a jury of a defendant's guilt, prosecutors rationalize that a lighter sentence is better than no conviction, and no sentence, at all.

In the Preppie Murder case in New York City in 1987, the killer, Robert Chambers, was allowed to plead guilty to first-degree manslaughter as the jury, deciding whether or not he was guilty of murdering young Jennifer Levin, entered its ninth day of deliberations.

Linda Fairstein, the New York City assistant district attorney prosecuting Chambers, allowed this plea bargain because the jury process appeared to be breaking down and the result could easily have been either a mistrial or a hung jury. Fairstein didn't think Jennifer Levin's parents could go through the torment of another trial; neither did they.

Chambers's defense attorney, Jack Litman, obtained for his client not the lengthy sentence for first-degree manslaughter but the five to fifteen years generally given for second-degree manslaughter.

DANCING WITH THE MASTERS OF DEATH

Ironically, while untold numbers of single men and women can't seem to meet the right person or can't sustain meaningful relationships, men convicted of murder appear to attract women easily. As a matter of fact, some murderers seem to be so attractive that women flock around them, vying for their attention.

The men are generally charming and seductive. "These guys are incredible con men," said social worker Lois Lee, who works with teenage prostitutes in California and played a role in assisting investigators in the Hillside Strangler case. "I get letters from them; they want to start a correspondence with my kids—which I don't let them do."

"These guys are never without women," said one law enforcement officer. In psychiatric jargon, some murderers, the charmers, fit into the *psychopathic* or *narcissistic* categories. "These men have a great appeal to women," said forensic social worker Dr. Warren. "Whether these men are criminals or whether they're heads of corporations, they have a charming, powerful quality that draws people to them."

These charismatic murderers are totally different from the type of killer who murders his wife or girlfriend. In a three-page letter to this writer in November 1989, Hillside Strangler Bianchi was disarming, intelligent, articulate. In suggesting a collaboration on a book about his life, he wrote: "It should come as no surprise that I'm in the process of writing my story—from childhood to the present. . . . Thus

far, five chapters are completed, along with a pref-
ace. . . . Although I received A's in English classes here,
I'm no experienced nor professional writer. My chapters are
rough, but truthful and require a creative, albeit honest,
continuing touch."

Charismatic murderers are expert con men. Francine,
married to a convicted killer, said: "Ninety-nine percent of
the men are narcissistic. They have no depth, no understanding of how to survive in today's world, which is one reason
why they are where they are, and they are learning nothing
from the experience. But a lot of them are pretty adept con
artists." (Her husband, of course, is different: "He has
never, ever, lied to me, not one time.")

"They don't call them con men for nothing," said
Maria. Murderers are often so captivating, women forget
why they are in prison. Lorraine met an inmate through her
brother, who was also in prison. She married him because
he had an "almost hypnotic hold on me. . . . The guys in
prison really know how to get what they want."

Tommy Trantino, in a New Jersey state prison for the
1963 murder of two police officers, is "tall—six feet one
inch—muscular, long haired, rugged, the cowboy type," according to Paramus, New Jersey, police chief Joseph Delaney. More than a decade ago, when he was on death row,
Trantino was visited by his attorney and the attorney's wife,
Charlee. "Charlee appeared to be the demure, silent, small,
soft-spoken type," said Delaney. Her lawyer husband "was
almost a male likeness of Charlee," quite different from
Tommy Trantino in appearance and demeanor.

Although he was convicted of murder, Trantino wooed
and won Charlee. Delaney said he believed Charlee and her
husband must have split up over Trantino, whom he described as "glib, a great con artist, very manipulative, with
a striking look about him." There is no question in Delaney's
mind that Charlee was swept away by Trantino's charm. "He
could be a pied piper, he's that charming."

Yet Trantino's crime was particularly heinous. As Delaney tells it, one night in 1963, while sitting in the Angel Lounge in Lodi, New Jersey, celebrating a robbery, Trantino encountered two policemen who were responding to a noise complaint. The first man into the bar was a sergeant. When he didn't return, his partner, an unarmed rookie, went in after him. Both officers were made to strip, then were pistol whipped and shot, said Delaney.

"The most obvious person that Charlee—strictly by theory and thinking of her as diminutive and easy to intimidate—the most obvious person she'd be attracted to, is someone who is macho, good looking and dangerous—Trantino," said Delaney. According to the police chief, Charlee believes that her husband is rehabilitated—but also that he never committed the crime of which he was convicted.

A columnist for the Wilkes-Barre, Pennsylvania, *Times Leader,* Steve Corbett, commented, "She considers Tommy to be sensitive and caring. . . . She is impressed with his painter/poet/author status." Trantino has had a book of poetry, *Lock the Lock,* published.

One of the most attractive qualities of men who have killed is their ability to focus on another person, to *really* listen to what she is saying. According to psychoanalyst Dr. Carl Rotenberg, men in prison are "the best psychologists in the world" because they spend most of their time watching people and reading them. Out of necessity, out of their need to survive, they learn this skill on the streets and once in prison, perfect their ability to interpret facial expressions, voices, and body language.

When a man who has killed focuses this way on a woman, it's often the first time, for her, that anyone has paid her that much attention. For the murderer, it's done out of necessity, out of a need to survive. He has to learn all he can about this woman as soon as possible, to find out if she's friend or foe. But for the woman, it feels like a loving touch; the romance for which she yearns begins with his closeness, his constant eye contact, his hanging on her every word.

MURDERERS MARRYING

Until 1989, New York State did not allow lifers—murderers, for the most part—to marry. But on May 26 of that year, U.S. district judge Neal McCurn in *Langone* v. *Coughlin* overturned the New York law, calling it arbitrary and irrational. "The right to marry in a prison setting is a fundamental one," he wrote in his decision.

A large number of inmates and free women agreed with him. During the latter part of 1989, the New York State prison system was inundated with requests for marriages between convicted killers and their long-term girlfriends. Richard Langone, thirty-three, an inmate serving fifteen-to-life for a drug-related murder when he was eighteen, was one of the first to take advantage of the new law. "Marriage is important for someone in prison. It makes a person feel like he's got something," Langone told Associated Press writer Marc Humbert.

Sure. He has a friend, a supplier of money, food, gifts, and sometimes drugs and other contraband, a lover, a wife, a companion, a helpmate—everything a man serving endless years in prison would want, short of his freedom.

"The men need an advocate on the outside, otherwise they're dead," said Jeanette Erickson, a strong supporter of prison reform in Pennsylvania where her brother is jailed. For a man doing time for murder, having a woman on the outside is like a gift from heaven. She is a positive influence with parole boards, a sure way to secure a furlough or short visit home, even proof that he is "normal."

But the convicted murderer is not normal. No matter the specifics of his crime, he can never really be described as just a regular fellow. And a relationship between such a man and his woman on the outside is never regular and ordinary. In fact, it has more in common with the fantasy of romance novels and soap operas than it does with real-life love and marriage—despite protestations to the contrary made by the women interviewed for this book.

Francine has a real marriage, not a prison marriage. Charlie, her husband, a convicted murderer, feels that way, too. They are special, different, not like the other prison couples. When she drives the two hundred miles to visit him, she puts her bills in an accordion folder beside her on the front seat. Telephone, mortgage, gas and electric, doctor, dentist, even the vet bill for her two cats who just had their rabies shots. During their visit, they talk about household business, and Charlie helps Francine make financial decisions. He understands her hardships. She expects of him the same consideration and input as if he were free. When it's time to leave, after five hours together, after shared junk food from the vending machines, after much holding hands and looking into each other's eyes, Francine gets into her car and puts her accordion file on the passenger seat. She drives the two hundred miles home.

Francine shows total denial of reality. She and her husband are *playing* at being married, as children do, because if the electricity is turned off in her house for nonpayment, she suffers, not her husband. The state always makes certain that inmates have heat, hot water, and the other basics.

THE WEDDINGS

Couples get married in prison waiting rooms, in chapels if they're lucky, in tiny offices. Sometimes, they're separated by glass windows. During some ceremonies, they can hold hands. In Colorado, maximum-security inmates can marry only by proxy unless a woman is pregnant.

Annette got married in a white stone Episcopal church in a small town in Colorado. She wore a long red-and-white Christmas dress to set off her dark hair and skin and carried two dozen red and white roses. Jack, the man she was marrying, was not allowed to be there, so his son stood in for him. Annette said "I do" to her new stepson. He didn't kiss her at the end of the ceremony and she didn't look at him with stars in her eyes.

During an interview for this book, Annette, whose husband, Jack, is doing life in a Colorado penitentiary for first-degree murder, said about her wedding: *"It was really romantic."* But in a 1987 first-person piece in a Colorado newspaper, she wrote: "[His] grown son from his first marriage stood in for his dad and said the vow. *It was hardly romantic* [emphasis added], but I wanted to have it in the church."

On May 27, 1978, Geraldine Harper, dressed in a yellow gown, married Nathaniel Grimes, Jr., imprisoned since 1968 for murder. The bride, "still clutching her yellow bouquet," went home alone after the ceremony, reported the June 1983 edition of *Ebony* magazine. After their marriage, Geraldine Harper Grimes worked at a kindergarten in Thomasville, Georgia, while her husband—who had spent more than three years on Florida's death row—served his sentence 180 miles away in Raiford, Florida.

October 23, 1989, a bright autumn day in upstate New York, is the wedding day of the most well-known jailhouse lawyer in New York State, and possibly in the country, Jerry "the Jew" Rosenberg. Jerry and Ella are married in the dreary visitors room of the prison where he is doing life for felony murder.

Jerry, in his fifties, his skin the dead gray that speaks of months, maybe years, in the hole—solitary confinement— is quiet. Ella, attractive, ebullient, about thirty, has her two little boys with her. She met Jerry in 1983 when she was studying at Syracuse University for a master's degree. This is her wedding, and no matter where the ceremony is, no matter that it's the institutional setting of a prison visiting room, she's dressed for it: a white silk dress, a veil and headpiece decorated with pearls, and white heels. Jerry wears his prison uniform of green shirt and pants.

The reception is a table strewn with paper wrappings of Ring-Dings and Twinkies, the junk food dispensed by the vending machines, and ashtrays filled with butts. Her little boys, bored, run around the room, careening into other tables. "Do you want Daddy to get in trouble?" Ella shouts to them repeatedly.

The prison superintendent comes in to congratulate the couple. Other inmates, sitting with their own visitors, look over at Jerry and Ella from time to time. This is clearly an occasion. Jerry is an unusual inmate. In 1967, he became the first person in New York to earn a bona fide law degree from behind bars. In 1974, he was the first prisoner permitted to represent a client in a jury trial. Stephen Bello, author of *Doing Life: The Extraordinary Saga of America's Greatest Jailhouse Lawyer,* calls Jerry the "most accomplished and successful jailhouse lawyer in the country." Bello believes in Jerry's innocence, that he was wrongly convicted for felony murder in connection with the homicides of two police officers.

After the low-key celebration in the visiting room, Jerry is returned to his cell. Ella drives home with her boys. Although they are married, it makes no real difference to either Jerry or Ella tonight. Or any other night. The prison has no facilities for conjugal visits.

CONJUGAL VISITS

Some of the rush to marry in New York State, and other states, has to do with nothing more complex than a desire on the part of the inmates to have sex with a woman. A Texas woman, married to a man convicted of killing five people, writes: "Of course, some of these relationships don't have much depth either. I can tell you in two words why there has been a sharp rise in the number of proxy marriages in the TDC [Texas Department of Corrections] within the last two years—contact visits!"

As of January 1989, the *Corrections Yearbook,* put out by the Criminal Justice Institute, states that conjugal visits— also called trailer visits—are allowed in nine states. During these visits, a married couple is left alone for a number of hours, or even days. They can enjoy sex in the privacy of a trailer or special housing unit set aside for that purpose. Many babies have been born out of these unions. A pilot program was set up in 1983 at the Mississippi State Penitentiary that allows inmates to have as many as forty-two conjugal visits a year. "If an inmate is in good standing and behaves well, he can spend more time with his wife than the warden can spend with *his*," said a prison official quoted in *Ebony* magazine.

Sex during a contact visit is incredibly intense, romantic, and passionate. Think about it! A man is imprisoned for murder and hasn't made love to a woman in five, ten, fifteen years. Then he meets, courts, and marries a loving, more-than-willing woman—and boom! There he is, having sex with a woman finally, again, at long last! What could be more dramatic, more romantic and erotic, for both the man and the woman?

Conjugal visits, in addition to providing a sexual outlet, also serve to solidify and strengthen the bond between couples. If the woman becomes pregnant, the relationship becomes even more stabilized.

Judy is married to a man who has killed twice. She has also had a child with him. The State of California says he's in for life with no chance of parole. Judy married Roberto even though he knifed a man to death during a poolroom/bar fight and even though it was his second murder. They've been married seven years now, and their child, born as the result of conjugal visits, is five. Judy believes Roberto's sentence might be reduced to life *with* the possibility of parole because he is married and has a family. "He [originally] pleaded guilty to first-degree murder because his attorney told him a jury would give him death." Judy and her child live on hope, waiting for Roberto to be freed.

LIFE WITHOUT SEX

The majority of convicted killers and their wives are not allowed conjugal visits. But even the nine states that provide these visits place limitations on them. If a murder is sex related—like the killings committed by the Hillside Stranglers—the inmate is not allowed contact visits. In still other prisons, there are simply no facilities.

For one reason or another, the majority of women interviewed for this book have never had sex with their husbands or boyfriends. A very small number of women reported having a stolen sexual encounter or two. Despite this lack of sex—or perhaps because of it—these women remain monogamous.

"Once we did [have intercourse]. . . . They had a park setting, and they had picnic tables, and you could barbecue and stuff like that. The tables were very far apart, and obviously there were people there to monitor you, but they didn't constantly patrol. . . . It was very, very unsatisfying, obviously, because it was furtive . . . frightening . . . terribly secretive. It was not anything that you could enjoy or be relaxed about."

Francine and Charlie never had sex again although they have been married for more than a decade "because of . . . the potential for being shamed. . . . I don't want that again. Can you imagine, at my age, having someone come upon you, and being caught in that—and then being shamed and scolded?"

The women interviewed, who love men with whom they cannot have sexual relations, all said they were having a hard time with it but could handle it. "I think it's an awful, awful, awful burden," said one woman. "It's very difficult to deal with because obviously if you love a man, you have tremendous longing to be with him and that is always frustrating. So it means that the suffering is terribly acute because you're always unfulfilled." None of the women interviewed for this book said they would consider having sex in a public waiting room.

They go through humiliation and pain and suffering—indeed these are central to their love as we'll see later—but before they begin their relationships, none of these women know what lies ahead. None are aware of how difficult these relationships will be. They meet the men, fall in love—then find out.

Teddi: A Case of Salvation

"He always went one step further"

THE FUNERAL

Teddi was in turmoil. Sitting in a front pew near her parents, she felt alone even though the church was filled with friends and relatives. Her stepbrother Artie was gone and with him, her sense of safety and security. Although ten years older and worlds apart, Artie was always willing to take the time to listen. No one else listened to Teddi the way he did.

Birds sang and the sun shone outside the church. But to the ten-year-old girl, the sun had set and would never rise again. Artie, her hero, her prince, was dead of a heroin overdose at the age of twenty. The year was 1957.

Sitting there, waiting for the mass to begin, Teddi remembered how she didn't believe it when her mother said Artie was dead—until she saw the blood coming out of his mouth and nose. She felt the pain of abandonment over and over. "I always wanted Artie to take me everywhere. I really resented him leaving."

The family mourned Artie, surrounded by relatives, neighbors—and police. Theirs was a tough, inbred, Italian neighborhood in Jersey City where gangs held sway, secrets were kept to the death, and crime was a way of life. The police had been in and out of the house, checking Artie's body, looking for drugs, trying to find out if the overdose was accidental. Three days later, the entire close-knit neighborhood turned out for the funeral.

Sitting in church, Teddi remembered when Artie came to live with her family after his own mother died. He was the one who listened to her when she could no longer stand the chaos, the noise, the mob scene, in her house. She would go to Artie, who would point to her temples and say—"The ticket out is there."

But Artie himself used a different route—heroin. Although the family was constantly disrupted because of his addiction, his drug use also provided Teddi a refuge of sorts. Their closest times were when he was stoned, nodding out on a fix. "He would be sitting on the couch and I knew the look. . . . He seemed so happy and at peace and I had the most fun. . . . I looked for that . . . more than the other way [when] he was very troubled, very angry, very violent."

Artie's death meant the end of comfort for Teddi. No one else would be her friend the same way. She squirmed in the pew. The community was waiting, too. Even the priests had to wait for the young lords of the neighborhood—the gang members—to say their good-byes to Artie, lying in his open coffin.

Suddenly, a thrill went through the church: Marty was there. "Everything seemed very tense at that moment. No one knew how Marty was going to react." Artie's best friend, Marty, a gang leader, was an important person in the neighborhood, a "knight in shining armor, always gallant, very noble, but also a rebel. . . . If someone made a dare—like climb out on the roof—Marty would be the one to climb out on the roof—and then hang off. He always went one step further. . . . He needed to be noticed, to stand out from the crowd."

The hushed crowd watched Marty walk up to Artie's coffin and listened as he talked softly to his friend. Then Marty "cried like a baby. I thought what a strong friend he was." The toughest of the young toughs was not afraid to show his vulnerability.

Afterward, Teddi stood outside the church with the other children. Marty emerged, a leader flanked by his gang members. He walked over to Teddi, touched her hair, and said, "Everything will be okay, kid." Suddenly, she believed it would be. Her faith in Marty was total; Teddi knew he wouldn't say anything that wasn't true. "I felt, all of a sudden, protected again, and I felt that I had a piece of Artie back."

Once again, Teddi had a knight to save her from the sordidness of life. She held on to the talisman of Marty's words and his touch for the rest of her life.

IN PRISON

It is three decades later. Teddi and Marty sit in the visiting room of a maximum-security correctional facility, holding hands, looking into each other's eyes. Her long blond hair streaming down her back, blue eyes lit with love, Teddi comes alive. A sleek, handsome man, Marty strokes Teddi's hair. "No one has beautiful hair like my girl," he says. She relishes his touch, almost purring under it. Her eyes make love to him as her hands caress his.

Teddi and Marty married in 1989. For Marty, convicted of murdering a sheriff's officer and serving twenty-five years to life, the marriage means possible conjugal visits and a committed relationship. For Teddi, it means the man she has loved all her life is finally hers.

Marriage to Marty is the realization of years of fantasizing for Teddi. Through two earlier marriages, the birth of four children, throughout her entire adult life, Teddi dreamed about Marty since that long-ago day when he touched her hair and promised her it would be okay. Teddi does not allow Marty's murder of a policeman to interfere with her love.

DEATH ON THE PARKWAY

According to an interview this writer had with a police official on the scene and the official report of the incident, it was a quiet, cloudy autumn Tuesday in 1974. No unusual events had been reported over the radio, so Mike Farrow, a Bergen County sheriff's officer on patrol, parked in a U-turn area near a rural parkway and watched for speeders. Two cars drove by. They followed each other closely on the nearly empty road, almost as if they were driving in tandem.

Farrow pulled next to the first car and saw a man and a woman in the front seat. Then he dropped back and looked at the second car, a Cadillac. A man in his forties was driving, and a younger man was in the backseat. He signaled the Cadillac to pull over onto the right shoulder. When the driver went for his license, he came up empty-handed. Farrow ordered the driver out of the car, patted him down, and told him to stand at the rear of the Cadillac. Farrow then turned to the dark-haired, nervous-looking man in the backseat: Martin Simmons, thirty-seven—the Marty of Teddi's dreams, out of jail for only a short time after having served a three-year term for armed robbery.

Of the two slightly different versions of what occurred next, the first can be found in court and police records, and the second is Teddi's story, told to her by the man she loves. The outcome of both versions is the same: Mike Farrow was shot and killed by Martin Simmons. In his old neighborhood, people on the street expressed no surprise that Marty Simmons had killed. A heroin addict, Marty had lived on the edge for years. This time, though, Marty had gone too far out on the limb; it had broken, throwing him to the ground.

THE OFFICIAL VERSION

The police version of Farrow's death is the story of an un-suspecting cop gunned down by an escaping armed robber. Simmons, two other men, and a woman had driven to a rural part of New Jersey to rob an electronics store. They took $400 in cash and a cache of valuable equipment.

They were driving south toward Jersey City when Officer Farrow noticed them. After he pulled the Cadillac over and dealt with its driver, he went to check Simmons, in the backseat with his bush jacket next to him. Suddenly, Simmons pulled a .25-caliber automatic from a pants pocket and fired once at the policeman, who then pulled out his own gun and started backing up. He kept backing up, firing once at Simmons from the road, and again from the median. Farrow collapsed in the northbound lane, never having hit his target.

Marty and his accomplice jumped in the Cadillac and took off. Moments later, two passing off-duty state employees saw the downed officer and called for help. Several miles away, the Cadillac tried to drive around a long line at the tollbooth of the Garden State Parkway. When the toll collector yelled at them to stop, they crashed through a wooden barrier and took off down a side road. In a matter of minutes, the dead sheriff's officer and the runaway Cadillac were linked and the hunt was on.

Marty and his accomplice drove on, then stole a two-door 1968 black Ford at gunpoint from a woman. In Pearl River, they dumped the Ford and took a cab. When the cab was stopped at a roadblock set up by the Bergen County Sheriff's Office, one of the officers saw a gun butt sticking out of a pocket of Simmons's bush jacket.

The two men were arrested and held without bail. In 1975, Marty Simmons was tried and sentenced to twenty-five years to life for second-degree murder. He also received concurrent sentences for robbery and criminal possession of a weapon.

TEDDI'S VERSION

"I could have told you when I was fifteen years old that Marty would have ended up in prison someday—either that or dead. . . . It was the road he was taking, the lifestyle, the drugs." Marty turned to heroin and crime because they were a way of life for many in the neighborhood. A junkie when he went into prison the first time, Marty came out with a worse addiction. "I remember seeing him two days after he came out, and the only thing that changed was that he was walking the streets. He was the same person, still into drugs. Marty was into drugs from the time he was thirteen."

In prison, Marty had no trouble getting high since drugs, like alcohol and other contraband, are easily obtainable for the right price from certain inmates or guards. Released after his robbery term, he went to a walk-in health center in the neighborhood looking for rehab but was turned down; the officials told him there was a conflict in treating him since he was on parole.

A broke, ex-con junkie, unable to support his habit and unable to get treatment, Marty agreed to a friend's plan to rob an electronics store. But the robbery was postponed a day, and Marty, needing a fix, was "pretty well strung out" when the heist finally took place. After the robbery, with about $250,000 worth of goods in their possession, the three men were on their way back to their own turf when fate stepped in: Mike Farrow, looking for speeders.

Teddi doesn't believe Farrow's was a routine check. "The policeman did not log the stop. . . . The lights weren't on. He just pulled up next to them and waved them over. . . . The indication we have is that he was looking for a payoff." Farrow behaved in an odd manner. "He took a wallet and put it in his back pocket, which is something that a cop never does. They never touch the wallet at all." Then Farrow reached for Marty's jacket. "This is something else that they never do. They never touch the clothing on a routine traffic violation." Since Marty knew the gun and handcuffs he had used in the robbery were in its pocket, he grabbed for the jacket.

"I believe there was something else on the cop's mind. They were not speeding. . . . We have some evidence he had a drinking problem. He had never progressed career-wise.

"At this point, the officer started backing up, went for his gun. Marty pulled [his] gun out of his jacket pocket and then everything happened. Marty shot once, thought he grazed him, jumped in the car, and left. Marty didn't even know he was dead." Farrow fired twice, shattering a window on the car. Marty was unaware he had killed the officer until he stopped in a bar for a drink and heard the news on television.

"Marty had never shot a gun before in his life; he couldn't believe he had even hit him." His earlier conviction for armed robbery was based on his threatening a convenience-store clerk with a toy gun. "Marty is really not, believe it or not, a violent person. He didn't use a real gun. As much as he had a reputation for being a tough guy or a fighter, he was a hands kind of guy—a fair fight, one-on-one guy."

Marty would not intentionally have killed Farrow, according to Teddi. "That was always the thing with Marty. . . . [When] they stole a car from this woman who had a baby with her, she commented in court that Marty was very gentle with the baby. [His partner] wanted to tie them up, and Marty wouldn't allow it. There were always the dos and don'ts with Marty."

Marty only had the gun with him "for control," never intending to use it. "Actually, knowing Marty the way I know Marty, he would probably do everything he could not to shoot first. As a matter of fact . . . Marty first tried to talk to [the deputy] and said to him, 'Calm down. Why does one of us have to hurt you?' "

But Marty was a survivor and would do anything to live. Teddi assumes her man's back was against the wall and so can understand his killing the policeman. "They were both

attacking each other. . . . Marty could have died just as easily. . . . I'm grateful that it wasn't Marty and I'm sorry it
was [Farrow]."

LIFE BEFORE MARTY

Teddi rebelled against her family starting at about age
twelve. The women in her family, except for her aunt Olivia,
saw her as bad, calling her "a devil," saying, "Oh, she will
never fit in." With the exception of her great-grandfather,
the men took little notice of her. After all, in the 1950s, girls
were not very important.

Her father "was here for the boys, but not for [me]."
Busy with his work, with homing pigeons on the roof and
the social club down the block, he had no time for his
daughter. Her mother stabilized the family, always there
in the background, cooking, cleaning, ministering to the
children.

Every day, Teddi ran to an alley where she and a friend
had a secret place for sheltering stray animals. Teddi would
never ask her parents to allow her to keep a pet; there was
barely enough money to feed the family of eight.

Her father, whom she idolized when she was very little,
fell from her good graces, and when she entered her teens,
Teddi could barely tolerate him. "There was a point in my
life where I really turned off to him. He was a real creep."
She was disappointed because he either couldn't or didn't
want to provide well for his family. "I thought he was just
terrible. He didn't care about nothing. He wasn't flexible at
all. . . . Jobs he could have had, he turned down because
he wasn't going to have a boss. No one was going to tell him
what to do."

Teddi cared about status. When she was very young,
the neighborhood was composed mainly of immigrants, but
later, she was envious of the new people moving in who had
money to spend. "Before that, all of us were waiting from
paycheck to paycheck. . . . I hated the fact that my family

were immigrants. . . . I just wanted to be American with money and two cars and that sort of thing."

Her father, Joseph, drank. But then all the men drank. It was part of their way of life, like the social club. He "didn't really talk to you. . . . There was no big relationship one way or the other. If he didn't come home, I don't think I would have noticed it for quite a while." And yet, the house revolved around him. "We ate when Dad came home. Everything was for when he was going to be around."

Teddi felt abandoned by her father. "He wasn't coming to the school project, wasn't going on the trip, wasn't doing the things that some of the other kids' fathers seemed to be doing." He was not in her life, either emotionally or physically. "He was just not there for me. . . . A little girl goes to her father for protection and he sold me out.

"I was the middle child. I was expected to tolerate more pain, more disappointment." She was also the only girl. Alone and unprotected in a chaotic family and a tough neighborhood, Teddi turned to her stepbrother Artie for safety and security because she related more to him than she did to her brothers; they seemed to be more like their father while Artie, maybe because he was a junkie, was different. When Artie died, she felt more alone than ever.

Two other relatives who supported her when she got into trouble and encouraged her individuality and rambunctious spirit, an aunt and her grandfather, died also. By the time she was in her early teens, Teddi had developed an "abnormal fear of death."

She walked around feeling like an outcast in her own family. Told constantly that she was not "falling into place," she also avoided school as much as possible. Teddi, at thirteen, was confused about her developing sexuality and the mixed messages she got from her mother and other relatives—and from Susan, a prostitute who lived upstairs.

Although her family strongly disapproved of the sexual permissiveness of the sixties and warned Teddi to remain a virgin until she married, they rented out an upstairs apartment to a prostitute. This woman taught Teddi about sex.

Assertive and self-confident, Susan was the only successful businesswoman Teddi knew.

Teddi began to visit Susan often, and what she was told by this streetwise hooker contradicted the romantic notions she had grown up on. Teddi's fantasies had been created by the idealistic movies and big-band music of the forties, her parents' era. But she abandoned romance when she found out what it led to: sex. Surprisingly, the seemingly contradictory views of sex she received from Susan and from her relatives sustained each other. Both were based on the concept that sex is for men only, that women consent solely to gain men's approval, that women who engage in sex before marriage are tramps. The difference was the family didn't approve of tramps but to Susan, all women were whores, especially wives, and if you were going to be one, you might as well get paid for it. Everyone told Teddi men would use her.

To the still-innocent girl, Susan described harsh, violent sexual acts in graphic detail. She told Teddi these acts would be done to her, with or without her consent. She taught Teddi that if she gave in, she should be paid for it, that money would make the sacrifice worthwhile.

"Any man I met also pretty much confirmed what Susan was saying. . . . They were shallow. It was physical, purely physical." Teddi gave up the idea of falling in love. Neither the rigid family rules nor the prostitute's distorted views left any room for a young girl's dreams.

One day when Teddi went upstairs to baby-sit for Susan's toddler, one of Susan's johns sat waiting, anxious to buy sex with a thirteen-year-old. "He sort of attacked me." Susan had arranged the whole thing, and although she stopped it eventually, seeing that Teddi was not cooperating, Teddi felt violated. But she never blamed Susan: "That was part of Susan's lifestyle. If she could have brought in more customers by having a young kid there, that would have been her. . . . She thought that I had the look for it . . . the body for it."

Sex equals profit, Susan told Teddi over and over. No

sense giving it away for free. Since Teddi could find no balance between the opposing but reinforcing viewpoints expressed by the prostitute and by her family, she finally gave up on sex altogether. "I decided, well, this must be it. So I'm just not going to bother. . . . And I really didn't." She dated during her teenage years but never became sexually involved. She was a virgin at eighteen when she met her first husband, Vincent.

Teddi decided to get married in order to finally experience sex. "All my friends were doing this already and I felt like a real oddball. . . . I could not get past the point of allowing myself permission to do it unless I was married." She felt guilty about her sexual feelings because of the strong Catholic anti-sex bias of her family. Teddi also had a somewhat twisted view of sex because of her exposure to Susan. "I hated the idea of it—all the details that were involved. . . . And as time went on, I saw Susan looking . . . horrible . . . trashy looking," as if what she did for a living were reflected in her face.

Feeling guilty and afraid, Teddi married Vincent. "I finally got enough nerve to step over the line and try it, and this is what I come up with. It was the worst experience of my life. I was ashamed to tell anybody because I started looking at it like I was failing."

Vincent had a problem. Anytime he approached Teddi sexually, he became either physically sick or violent. Ironically, the man Teddi had chosen to initiate her into sex was himself incapable of normal sex. "The psychiatrist told me later he was a latent homosexual and extremely violent." Vincent was not interested in women.

On their honeymoon, they traveled to Virginia where Vincent's racehorses were stabled, checking into a hotel near the racetrack. But there was no passionate honeymoon. "A few nights went by and there was nothing. He would either get very drunk and go to sleep or he had to go check the horses." She just knew something was wrong with *her*.

Vincent told her that his inability to consummate their marriage was "very common," but Teddi didn't believe him.

She also had no one to turn to. "Do I go to the old Italian ladies who have no concept of their sexuality at all? Or do I go to Susan, who's going to say, fine, go to the racetrack, get the money, buy the clothes. You're doing better."

Teddi finally went along with the hooker's imagined advice. She wore the clothes, drove the car, spent the money. At eighteen, she was impressed with it all and just shoved aside her doubts and fears. Except that she had to take pills to "numb the whole situation."

The fighting started when Vincent demanded Teddi do his laundry, clean the house, play wife. The first time he hit her, she left him. But she came back; the arguments kept escalating and they split up again.

One day Teddi, living in a furnished room in Jersey City and working as a waitress, was kidnapped by Vincent and his friends, who took her for a ride. She called Vincent a "pathetic cripple" and he went crazy, using her like a punching bag. When one of the other men pulled out a gun, Teddi wasn't afraid. "I was very young, but I was very tired of life."

At that moment, she realized it couldn't get any worse. She was facing death and out of that came a newfound strength. "It was almost like a light switch that went on for me." She fought back until, battered and bruised, they dropped her off in her old neighborhood. She went to her parents' house where, true to form, her father lashed out at her for failing in her marriage. "He thought that I wasn't behaving like a wife should behave. . . . He blamed me, more or less, for my husband's violence because I didn't fall into place."

Two more violent episodes occurred. A friend, "a crooked cop," tried to rape Teddi, but she resisted very hard. "Once it got into the fight, he got more into the beating, I think, than the actual sex." Grabbing a statue off a nightstand of Jesus wearing a crown of thorns, Teddi hit her would-be rapist over the head and got away from him.

Months later, she almost died at Vincent's hands. She returned to their old apartment to pick up their dog, but

Vincent came home before she could leave. "There was no fire escape and no way out. I knew that I was caught. . . . He hit me and I hit my head on the sink. . . . The next thing I knew, he was standing over me with a rifle." Vincent shot and killed the dog. Neighbors, hearing the shot, called the police.

Teddi had tried to make her marriage work, in part because of her mother. "I kept wanting to prove to her that I was going to make everything better and I was going to fall into place. I was going to be like every other wife." And because of her father. "He believed that a wife should know when to shut up." He told Teddi she had not learned that lesson and was a failure at being a wife.

Determined to prove her father wrong, Teddi went directly from her first disastrous marriage into a relationship with a different kind of man—who also turned out to be violent. Peter appeared stable, steady, and safe. When Teddi married him at twenty-one, she already felt old and welcomed the chance to have a normal life, a solid marriage. Peter, thirty, was a good provider and loved Teddi. "Peter was the way out . . . the way of calming everyone down and saying, okay, she's going to get normal." A fireman, he saw life as black or white, right or wrong. He expected of Teddi what her family expected: be a good wife, cook, have children, don't make waves.

She was pregnant when they got married and thrilled about it. (It was her second pregnancy. A first ended in a miscarriage when Vincent kicked her in the stomach.) The baby would be all hers, someone to love whom no one could take away. Although Teddi had some thoughts of raising the baby alone, she talked herself into marrying Peter. "I thought, you're doing it again. You're not falling into place. . . . Give this baby a father and a home."

During their eighteen-year marriage, they had four children. While the marriage did not live up to the romantic fantasies of Teddi's youth, it was relatively calm until Peter's drinking got out of hand. He had always been a drinker, but Teddi expected men to drink. Actually, Peter was very much

like Teddi's father: "In opinions, whether political or traditional, a Sicilian. . . . Everything from the same foods to
the same outlook on life."

Peter drank more and more and finally began to beat
their children. Teddi, who had started working selling sportswear in a department store, was often not home and didn't
know about the beatings. She was aware, though, that her
husband didn't want her to work. Working outside the home
was not acceptable in a good Sicilian wife. "I wasn't there,
so he took it out on the kids." Teddi called it a career. Peter
called it desertion. The children, nine, seven, five, and one
when the beatings started, didn't tell their mother. One day,
arriving home early, Teddi found the baby unconscious from
being thrown against a wall. "I packed up the kids and moved
out." She began divorce proceedings.

For some time, Teddi had been aware that her marriage
wasn't working. "The whole thing I was living was a lie. My
relationship with him, what I was pretending to be with the
kids, was a lie, all of it." She was not a good wife; she could
not fall into place. It was time to start being herself.

She wanted to raise the children on her own, live her
own life. Conveniently, she had just been given a raise and
made supervisor of the sportswear department. "I was going
to take control totally. I started becoming more successful
in the work I did; I became secure."

MARTY

Throughout her life, Teddi had a love that, fed by her fantasies, grew to mythic proportions: Marty. "In the back of
my mind was always Marty. When my children were born
in the hospital, I resented my husband or his family walking
in when I was holding the baby, fantasizing that it was my
and Marty's baby."

In 1985, Teddi's mother, Christina, was dying in a hospital bed. Grab life instead of simply letting it drift by, Christina told her daughter. Get some happiness for yourself, she

said. The older woman was aware of Teddi's unspoken love for Marty. Write to him, she said. Even though Marty is doing life for murder, I'll be your go-between; I'll accept his letters for you, said Christina.

Christina liked Teddi's husband but knew their marriage was doomed. How could a husband compete with a legend?

"Marty was the one we all looked up to. . . . He was a leader . . . in good things as well as bad." Marty had charisma, charm, grace. He was a leader and everyone in the neighborhood respected him; some revered him. "Even now, you go back to the neighborhood, a lot of the younger kids know that I'm with Marty, and they've heard stories of Marty. . . . Guys in their twenties . . . sit there and ask me questions like they're talking about some legend."

Like other gang members, Marty had a strong code of ethics that he followed, a standard of honor. But there were two sets of rules: one for neighborhood people, friends, family, and a second set for outsiders. "What applied to us didn't necessarily apply to the girls in the next neighborhood." It certainly didn't apply to police.

"He was from the old school, very old-fashioned. . . . If you were in a bad section of town, he would always get you home." To Teddi, Marty was Robin Hood; he did "bad" things but he was really "good." Both Marty and her stepbrother Artie "were bad inside. They robbed. They lied. They did drugs. But . . . they would defend you to the death. They were protective of people they cared about. But if they didn't care about you, they could be as cold as they could be."

Teddi and Marty had dated before she married Vincent but as friends only. They never developed any kind of romantic relationship because Teddi was young and afraid and wanted to become a good wife while Marty was attracted to a deviant lifestyle. They had never had the time or the opportunity to love each other—or to make love either.

From her hospital bed, Christina instructed her daughter to sacrifice herself for Marty just as she herself had given up her life for Teddi's alcoholic, withdrawn father. "Everything was for my father. Her whole life was for him. My mother saw that I had the same thing for Marty that she had for my father, and that was the *total* acceptance of the man as is, the willingness to sacrifice."

Teddi felt ambivalent, though, because she had always been aware that Christina gave in to her husband in order to keep the peace. Christina even told Teddi that Joseph "didn't do right by her. He didn't do what he could have done. She felt he could have bent more and given more to her." But mother and daughter both felt sacrifice was a necessary ingredient in marriage: the wife's sacrifice. "I may not have agreed with certain sacrifices that my mother made for my father. But I certainly can see how it cemented their relationship more and more." In order to make her own life meaningful, Christina wanted her legacy of subjugation to continue into a second generation.

Teddi and Marty had the possibility of sharing something unique. "My mother said, 'I see a lot of the same qualities in the relationship, but you have to know who the man is, what he's capable of, but most important what he's not capable of—and love him just the same and accept that in him.' "

In this marriage of convicted killer and sacrificing woman, the woman would have to be the strong one. The strength to hold the relationship together, to fight the odds, would be Teddi's responsibility, not Marty's. Shortly after she left her husband Peter and began divorce proceedings against him, Teddi accepted her mother's legacy and wrote to Marty in prison, saying she wanted to visit him. It would mean changing the fantasy that had been playing in her head for almost thirty years. "I always looked at Marty as the protector and the savior. We reversed roles somewhere along the line."

Teddi was finally ready to become a good wife. She began visiting Marty in prison, building her life around him, organizing her work and children around prison visits. She could rid herself of her sense of failure if she could marry this man she had always loved, taking on the enormous burden of a relationship with a lifer. Teddi had challenged the rules for being a good girl, but nothing had worked out; her failures made her feel worthless. "I became a disappointment. I got a real hang-up over that. . . . Everything I tried to do, they're telling me it's not going to work, it's not going to work. I said, yes, it is. I'm going to do this. And then it didn't work. I felt like a total failure." Now, by marrying Marty, she would succeed.

LOVE AND MARRIAGE

There were no flowers at the wedding. No cake. No music. No guests. Teddi's children, who made the long trip from Brigantine to the New Jersey State Prison in Trenton to witness their mother's marriage, were forced to wait outside the prison. The wedding was a bit of business—no romance was allowed by prison officials. "The woman sat down; she didn't even bother standing. . . . We had wanted to exchange our own vows, and things like that. . . . We signed on the dotted line. . . . We left."

Teddi cried. "It was more of a sigh of relief. It was like they had to recognize our relationship." She was also reacting to the momentous occasion; she was legally marrying the man of her dreams, her handsome, dashing Sir Galahad. "I heard Marty saying the words and that was beautiful."

After the wedding, Marty was escorted back to his cell and Teddi had dinner with her children. Later, she and the children went to a hotel. "I'm sitting in the hotel, looking at the kids, and I kept saying, 'We're actually legally married.' So the kids ask me, 'What's next, Mom? What do we do next?' " So Teddi went on a honeymoon—with her children. She even took pictures.

Returning home, married but alone, knowing she would not see him for another week, after another long drive— one of hundreds she had made during the two years she had been visiting Marty in prison—Teddi knew she would sleep alone in bed that night and possibly for many more years.

Unfortunately for Marty and Teddi, New Jersey State Prison does not allow conjugal visits. That's okay, according to Teddi. "The physical intimacy takes on a different form. With Marty and I, we hold hands or we kiss. . . . Mentally you're allowing yourself to be physically intimate. That whole part of it for me is more mental. The physical, anybody can control."

All around them in the visiting room people are having intercourse or oral sex. ("If they can get away with it, they'll do it. . . . Men going inside a woman. . . . They just pull up her skirt and put it in. The women don't wear stockings; I don't know if they wear underwear. . . . Women would come in and sit on their laps," said another woman in love with a murderer.) But Teddi and Marty limit their physical contact to hand-holding and touching. "The Department of Corrections would like . . . to believe that we're animals, that Marty acts totally basically on instincts, that he has no control over himself, that any woman who would make a commitment to a man like this also must have similar problems. So I won't give them that."

Teddi said it's actually the guards who are the animals. "They sit up on chairs and watch these people having sex. And I've seen men, guards, sitting there playing with themselves, watching."

In her years of visiting Marty, Teddi has seen all kinds of visiting-room sex. "Everything from clothes that open, Velcro zippers . . . If they can get a guard to allow them ten minutes in a closet . . . A lot of oral sex . . . I've seen people do it with Bibles in their laps. They look like they're really close together, but actually her legs are over his."

She and Marty talk, sharing private thoughts and plans and hopes. No Velcro zippers for them. "I'm not having sex because I would want to be alone with Marty. . . . I won't give the guards that. . . . The guards do share the same beliefs that we're trash. . . . But it's more than the guards, it's the system . . ."

Teddi cherishes her commitment to Marty, and even though she can't have sex with him, she would never be unfaithful. "I like the old ways. I like being married. I like being faithful to one person." She now shares some of the beliefs of the women in her family. "Having gone through the whole sixties thing, I prefer the guidelines. I'm more comfortable with them. And maybe I was then, [but] . . . I wanted to be like everyone else." The rules about sexuality that she was taught make her feel secure, and she has chosen to live by them.

THE CROSS

Teddi is reliving the sacrificial life her mother had with her father. By loving a convicted killer serving a life sentence, she denies herself a companion to live with. She denies herself an ordinary relationship that could include sharing household chores, finances, and child rearing. Trained to sacrifice by her mother, the Catholic Church, and a patriarchal society, she welcomes the cross she bears.

Teddi is steadfast. "To me, I don't care if he's [far away] or he's next door. I'm going to visit him. I'm going to be there. . . . Every minute of time he is doing, it's as if I am doing it as well. . . . My life is at a standstill. I live in a cubicle. I live in a cell. My life is on hold like his is." For her, sacrifice is necessary, as it was with her mother and father. "The sacrifice is strengthening our relationship, cementing the bond. I've chosen that; Marty never asked me."

SALVATION

Teddi talks of Marty as "the protector and the savior," of "willingness to sacrifice," of cells and cubicles, of her female relatives "preaching." Only by repenting can she receive salvation. Only by bearing a burden of some kind, her own cross, can she adequately be punished for her past behavior.

Her mother said, you must bear a woman's burden. You must sacrifice for your man.

Many woman who love convicted killers were raised in the Catholic religion; they need to suffer in order to feel saved. Teddi feels guilty for not being the girl she was supposed to be, for not satisfying the requirements of her family, for not living up to her father's expectations, for not "falling into place." She believes she still has to suffer in order to achieve salvation, not realizing how much she has already suffered in her life.

Raised on a diet of loss and emotional neglect, she married into brutality. At the hands of her father, she was belittled and neglected. At the hands of her first husband, she was beaten and nearly killed. At the hands of her second husband, she saw her children abused.

Now, Teddi has decided that her rebellious past didn't work for her so she is following in her mother's footsteps, throwing herself on the altar of sacrifice and giving up her individuality. But it's a pleasant sacrifice. She can nurture and give to the shining hero of her childhood. She views Marty as her savior with a Christ-like aura: an all-powerful legend, hero, protector.

The irony is that her savior is really her burden: Marty is her cross.

Teddi is a splitter, employing a defense mechanism common to borderline personalities. "A person looks at things as good *or* bad but can never see them as good *and* bad. Splitters see the world in black and white tones; they can't see the gray," said psychiatrist Neil Kaye, M.D.

"In splitting, the individual highly values some object or person, then shortly after devalues it. He or she idealizes an object or person, then does the opposite," explained psychiatrist Park Dietz, M.D.

Splitting is an attempt to protect the good object by separating its bad, aggressive aspects—by splitting them off. "It indicates a polarization, in which opposites—especially good and bad—can no longer be integrated," writes psychoanalyst Jessica Benjamin in *The Bonds of Love*. By separating the good and the bad, the good remains pure and does not get contaminated by the bad. It is clear that Teddi, like Maria in Chapter 1, must separate the "good" parts of the man she loves from the "bad"—the killer—parts.

Teddi also splits her father, seeing him as all bad when she was a child ("He sold me out"), but now, as an adult, viewing him as okay, saying she wishes they were closer. She splits Marty and her stepbrother Artie, describing them as very, very good to those they cared about and very cold to those about whom they didn't care. She splits her mother: Her mother was good and took care of Teddi, but at the same time, she wasn't really there for her.

"Teddi is very well defended from reality," said Dr. Kaye. "She denies a great deal of what went on in her past and what's going on in her life now." For example, she was matter-of-fact about Susan's attempt to enlist her in prostitution at the age of thirteen.

Teddi does not see a connection between the three men she has married although all are substance abusers who have committed acts of violence. Two of the three have shown they are capable of murder. (Remember her first husband's standing over her with the rifle?) Teddi is so used to violence, she may not recognize it when it's staring her in the face. Even her beloved Artie, when he wasn't stoned on heroin, showed a rage so powerful, it frightened her when she was a child.

Marty is a knight in shining armor ("I'm absolutely so proud of him"), which is far from reality. He has spent much of his life in jail, has been a heroin addict, and is convicted of killing a sheriff's officer.

As a child, Teddi was betrayed by everyone. Her alcoholic father. Her passive mother. Her prostitute friend. Her stepbrother Artie, her favorite uncle, and her grandfather betrayed her by dying. Even something that was all hers—her first pregnancy—was taken away when her husband kicked her. Teddi finally had four children, and when she thought they were being endangered, she said: Enough! The bottom line is you can't take my children. Kill me, hurt me, but don't touch my children.

After years of being abused, Teddi decided to take control of her life. She is part owner of a small clothing store now, raises her four children on her own, and has a relationship with a man who can't abuse her—because he is locked up, under someone else's control. Marty is the perfect man for Teddi. He romanced her in the old-fashioned way with flowers and poetry. He can't place sexual demands on her. Loving Marty allows Teddi to be finally complete. He is her burden, allowing her to be a sacrificing woman. But because she works and he's in prison, she also plays the role of the good husband who earns a living and is independent. She plays both man and woman.

"When people see me and Marty as a couple, it's sort of like a continuing circle. I can't see where I leave off and Marty begins. It's like this solid kind of ring; we read each other . . . he's the male me and I'm the female him. It's all a blend."

Teddi has finally fallen into place.

How Women Meet Men
Who Kill

*"I am not a thief, robber, burglar, sex
offender, drug dealer/user, con man,
or nut case"*

How do free women meet convicted killers? Certainly
not in ordinary ways. Women who love men who kill are
inventive and determined. With exceptions, such as Teddi,
and although they will deny it, they meet killers in prison
by actively seeking them out. They look for love in all the
wrong places—and they find it.

Free women—women on the outside—and men who've
been convicted of murder are separated by the steel and
concrete of barbed wire and prison walls. So first, a convicted
murderer must want to form a liaison with a woman on the
outside.

ADVERTISEMENTS

One of the most common methods an inmate uses to meet
women is to place a personal ad. No, a convict doesn't write
that he's committed murder and would like to meet a woman.

He omits details about the crime but uses certain buzz words in his ad to attract women.

> Lonely inmate wants to hear from anyone who likes to write, share ideas and feelings. Age, sex, race, are unimportant. Please write Box . . .

The key words here are *lonely* and *share.* Also, the inmate's reference to writing and sharing ideas and feelings gives the impression that he's sensitive and interested in communicating.

> 23-year-old prisoner of drug war seeks correspondence with WF 21 to 40, or anyone. . . . Augusta Correctional Center, Craigsville, Va.

This man is letting readers of the personals know he is most interested in meeting a white female considerably older than he is. But by adding "or anyone" he's admitting he's so lonely, he will correspond with anybody.

> Prisoner, 34, 5'8", 155 lbs., brown hair, hazel eyes, college grad, seeks woman 18 to 45 for friendship/exchange of political views. Enjoys music, art, sports, and animals. Would also like to work with writer concerning prison reform manuscript. . . .

In this ad, the prisoner writes that he has a wide range of interests, is bright and involved with issues of the day, including prison reform. Also, this ad, as did the one above it, appeared in *The Nation,* a weekly political magazine with an educated, politically liberal readership.

I answered the last ad, hoping to find out how many responses the inmate received and whether he ultimately met any of the women. Here's his response to my letter: "I believe I could supply you with the information you seek plus more, as I have had pen-pal relationships in the past. . . . However, what troubles me at the outset is your less than good faith means of contacting me. . . . The fact that you chose not to divulge your address . . . This is somewhat insulting as it implies that you fear me or at the very least, don't trust me. . . . This much I will tell you: I have been in state prison since 1976. I am not a thief, robber, burglar, sex offender, drug dealer/user, con man, or nut case."

This man ended his letter by wishing me good luck whether or not I sent him my home address—his prerequisite for providing me with information. His letter revealed that he was intelligent and could write well. Its tone, however, showed he was quickly trying to gain the upper hand and control any future correspondence between us. And despite his statement about what he was *not,* the New York State Department of Corrections revealed he had been in jail since 1976 for murder.

The personality revealed in this letter is a good example of the forceful, manipulative character displayed by many murderers who ultimately become involved with women on the outside.

Another inmate whose ad I answered accused me of trying to exploit him, but surprisingly, he ended his letter: "If you would like to visit, send me a photo of yourself in your next letter." In my letter, I had asked if he had had a girlfriend since he'd been in prison. He replied: "Why, [do] you want to be my girlfriend or something?" I had also asked what crime he'd been convicted of. He answered: "No use telling you about it. You are not helping me towards getting out of prison in any way."

Then he gave me a list of questions. I had written to him on a professional basis, telling him about this book and asking him specific questions about his ad and the responses to it. His questions to me, on the other hand, were quite personal: "Are you married? Have you ever visited anyone in prison before? Do you have a boyfriend? Do you have children? How much money do you intend to make on this book?"

I didn't answer this letter but he wrote again. He told

me he had received more than two hundred responses to his ad in *The Nation* with "still more coming in." The women who answered his ad "wrote quite a lot of nice things and sent photos." Not about to give up on *any* woman writing him for any reason, he ended his second letter by telling me he had placed my name on his approved visitors' list. He also included detailed directions to the prison and finally, named a date on which I could visit.

So with no encouragement on my part, this inmate set up an appointment to meet me despite the fact that I had not responded to his first letter. This shows how important a relationship with a woman on the outside is and the lengths to which some murderers will go to establish one.

Another inmate in a California prison wrote to me, saying he had no idea why women answered the ad he had put in a magazine: "I can't think of one sane reason to start a relationship with a prisoner. Pen pals are great for both sides, but why buy into failure?"

PEN PALS

Letters, old-fashioned and out-of-style in this age of the telephone, still have an important place in prisons. Since inmates can't use the phones, except on a restricted basis and then only to make collect calls, letters are their main artillery in their battle to meet women. Personal ads, pen-pal clubs, and letter writing sponsored by various prison advocacy groups are often the way convicted murderers meet women on the outside.

Although women are often hesitant to admit they are lonely enough to write to an inmate, untold numbers do it all the time. Many inmates who become pen pals are convicted murderers. They have the longest sentences and are the most desperate for a relationship because they know they will either never get out of prison or will be old when they do.

• • •

Alicia met her boyfriend through a writers' club. "We were both English majors and I was an English teacher at the time." She is a little embarrassed about this and usually tells people they met through a friend. She thinks it's humiliating that she wrote to an inmate she didn't know.

Alicia was single and hitting thirty when she got her first letter from Bill. She likes to think they would have gotten involved had they known each other on the outside. "We have a lot of common background. We're both college educated. We're the same age." They wrote, then talked on the phone. "I found him a very interesting individual and I wanted to meet him. . . . I don't think Bill had any idea of looking for a relationship. . . . But he would call periodically and say, come on and meet me.

"The more I got to know him, the better I liked him." But of course, she was not really getting to know Bill, only the image he presented to her—and her own idealized version of Bill. Her family and friends totally disapproved. "When I first corresponded with him, I was semi-involved with a couple of people. One was a cop. I told the cop [about Bill] and he was absolutely furious. He told me I was making a big mistake. He said those guys just don't do one wrong thing; they fuck up for a long time and then get caught. I was getting the same thing from everyone."

Alicia didn't listen. She accepted Bill's out-of-state collect calls for six months, but was hesitant when he urged her to visit.

Like so many women who love convicted killers, she had never been inside a prison. Alicia tried to resist her fascination with this convict whose situation had the potential for causing her serious hardship if she got involved. "I tried to control it for a while. At first, I told him I didn't want to write to him because I was afraid of getting involved. And he understood that and he just let it go, but I wrote back to him and—well, you make little steps and then it becomes more and more."

Finally, she made the twelve-hour drive to meet him.

"As a person, I liked him. . . . I found him intelligent. Politically, philosophically, we're very similar. . . . He's very positive. He's one of those power-of-positive-thinking people." She knew what he looked like from his pictures; his voice was familiar, too, so meeting Bill held no great surprises. But on that first visit, she was so uncomfortable in the prison environment, she didn't want to return. Quite against her will, however, Alicia had fallen in love—and was compelled to return to the prison, again and again. "You get into a relationship because you fall in love. . . . I wouldn't recommend to anyone to step into this life. It's a very difficult life. I stepped into it because I became very emotionally involved with him from the beginning."

For some women, the initial motivation to meet a murderer is political. When Elena was in her late thirties and a human rights activist, a friend asked her to write to a lonely convicted murderer on Louisiana's death row. His name was Terry. He was a good-looking man and had received many letters from women, including the infamous porn star Marilyn Chambers. Elena wrote, and later, she went to Louisiana to meet Terry. Although there was a better than twenty-year age difference—Elena was older—the unlikely pair fell in love and married in 1985. Their romantic passion lasted two years; then Terry was executed.

VOLUNTEERS

Women also meet murderers by volunteering to work in a prison. Amanda met Uri in 1986 when he was doing life in a Pennsylvania state prison and she had volunteered to help coordinate a prison NAACP chapter. Amanda doesn't know why she chose to volunteer on the prison committee; she was afraid of inmates, uncomfortable around prisons.

Uri was part of a small core group that regularly attended NAACP meetings, and he helped Amanda get over her initial discomfort with the prison scene. "I had never been inside a prison before. . . . The first time I went [inside], I was scared. . . . The first time I walked by [the inmates], I just stared straight ahead. I was a nervous wreck." This refrain is heard over and over among women who love convicted killers. And yet all of these women take that step into a prison.

From the very beginning, Amanda felt Uri was different. The tall, dark-skinned, Middle Eastern Uri "wasn't just another inmate." Amanda dismissed Uri's conviction. He had been found guilty of a contract murder. He and his partner sold illicit drugs and had hired a hit man to kill someone who had attempted to cheat them. "I didn't go into the prison looking for love. But as we kept seeing each other at the meetings, I kept thinking I wanted to get to know him better." They started writing so they could communicate privately—the meetings were too open.

Initially, their letters were friendly, "what I call on the up-and-up, like talking about our lives and our common interests. By December, I had decided that I would like to get to know him, so I had to decide if I was going to be a coordinator or stop." The NAACP had a rule that volunteers who became emotionally involved with inmates had to drop out. Amanda made the choice: "I stopped being a coordinator, and in January of 1988, I started going to visit him [on my own]."

Like Amanda, Dolores met her man when she and her first husband, both very involved in their church, decided they could best help humanity by working in a prison. Dolores worked with inmates who had absolutely no visitors at all. She began to write to one convicted murderer, Louis, who wanted to share letters with someone. That correspondence has lasted for more than thirteen years, through the dissolution of her first marriage, a second marriage, and the dissolution of that one also. During the first twelve years, there were no romantic overtones. "It was platonic. We have only become romantically involved in the last year." But there were always problems with the relationship, even when it was simply a friendship, because Dolores is white and Louis is black. Both their families objected.

Sometime after her first divorce, Dolores remarried and moved to another state, but she kept writing to Louis. Her second husband disapproved of his wife's friendship with a black inmate, but she risked his anger and disapproval. She felt she was essential to Louis's well-being since the only friends he had were Dolores and a few people he had met through other inmates. Dolores and Louis cared deeply about each other: "I was as important to him as he was to me." As his oldest friend, she could not stop writing to him.

"He had never had a friendship with a woman as long as he's had one with me. He had never been able to establish such a long-term relationship with anybody without having sex confuse the whole thing. It's been a very positive part of his life." She never expected their friendship to change to romance, although it had been "building up." After her second marriage ended, she moved back to her home state and began to visit Louis again. "I was pretty broken up about yet another failure. I went to see him, and when I saw how the visit was going—it was one of those I-need-you-to-console-me type things—I didn't want that to interfere with our friendship. I decided until I was able to put my life in perspective again, until I could be a positive visitor, we would just correspond. He agreed but told me he would always be there if I needed him."

They kept writing, though, and after a few months, "our letters started having a different tone to them. We were wanting to explore other emotions. It seemed mutual so I started visiting him again. From that first visit, I felt a spark and so did he, and every visit is a little bit better."

THE CRIMINAL JUSTICE SYSTEM

Women on the outside also meet murderers through the criminal justice system. Sometimes the women are in a courtroom as spectators during a trial or as jurors, police officers, lawyers, court officials. It is not uncommon for jurors to become fascinated with defendants since a trial creates a strange intimacy between the primary participants. Jurors in murder trials spend weeks, even months, listening to every detail of a defendant's life. Sometimes, if the right dynamics are in place, if she is susceptible, a juror may develop romantic feelings toward a defendant.

FRIENDLY INTRODUCTIONS

Sometimes well-meaning friends introduce women to killers, perhaps because they know a lonely inmate or because they feel their friend would benefit from the meeting. Often in these situations the friends making the introductions have their own ongoing relationships with inmates. Maria (Chapter 1) was introduced to her boyfriend by a woman who was herself married to an inmate.

Kay, a thirty-year-old woman who lives in the nation's capital, was introduced to her murderer/boyfriend because a friend thought she needed a new man. At the time, Kay was having serious difficulties with her boyfriend so a friend tried to set her up with Ruben, a convicted murderer serving a life sentence.

That Ruben was a murderer didn't place him out of bounds. "I talked to Diana and she said that there's this fine Rasta man down there that [I] must meet. She said he's nice looking. She knew I was having problems in my relationship." At first, Kay resisted the idea of replacing her boyfriend with a man imprisoned for murder. Then, increasingly unhappy, she called Diana. "I said, remember what you were telling me the other day? Let's do it."

Kay and Ruben wrote to each other, and when he sent Kay a photo, she was thrilled. "He was gorgeous! I just sat there and looked at the picture. That is going to be my husband one day. I'm going to marry this man." They arranged to meet. "I was so nervous. My legs were trembling. I was shaking. I waited a long time. This is the moment. I was a nervous wreck." Thunderstruck by Ruben's looks and presence, Kay was swept off her feet and committed herself immediately. When she thought about his life sentence, she felt sure it could not be true. "I felt like—oh, God, in my heart I feel he's not going to serve all that time."

WORKING WOMEN

Many social workers, nurses, teachers, journalists, psychologists, and women in other professions enter the prisons in the course of their work, and some fall in love with killers. A number of the women interviewed for this book work in these professions.

Mary met her husband, Al, in 1985 when they both worked in a mental hospital, she as an administrator, he as an inmate/staffer working in a special program. They became romantically involved a year later. She is white and he is black.

"He was one of many inmates who came to the hospital every day [to work] . . . and was considered a staff person. I was very impressed with the work he was doing with the patients and had noticed him over a period of time." Although he was convicted of murder, Al was in a minimum-security prison, received monthly furloughs, or home visits, and left the prison on a regular basis to work in the mental hospital or to umpire Little League games.

Mary liked Al's work long before she fell in love with him. One day, an extremely withdrawn patient agreed to go to therapy only after Al sat on the floor with him and convinced him. The patient, unfortunately, escaped and subsequently killed himself. "Al felt responsible. . . . [The patient] had . . . hung himself. . . . Al was devastated because he was always dealing with his own thoughts of suicide. People inside, their greatest fear is going crazy, killing themselves."

When Al talked about the patient's suicide with Mary, she became even more interested in him. "I realized this was someone I wanted to get to know better: his insight into his own situation, his commitment to helping other people, to taking something horrible and destructive that had happened in his own life and turning it into something constructive."

She was attracted to this seemingly sensitive, caring man who could work with mentally ill patients, draw them out, communicate with them. Drawn only to these qualities, Mary denied his crime and fell in love. Al's murder? Mary said his gun went off accidentally after he was shot by the owner of the store he was burglarizing. Al's victim, who tragically got in the way of the bullet, was a clerk in the store.

Mary never thought Al would serve his full term. "When we got involved, it was with the thought that in a matter of time, a few years, he would be out. But now, I don't know." The love she felt for Al was out of her control; it just happened to her. "I don't think you make the choice to pursue it. It ends up unfolding in front of you and you move with it."

Perhaps because social workers counsel murderers in prison, a few of them fall in love with "their" inmates. District Attorney Howard R. Relin, in Monroe County, New York, told about a social worker who loved and planned to marry convicted killer James R. Moore. "Moore committed one of the most notorious crimes in the state. He saw a young girl, followed her, killed her, and then raped her. He was already on probation for abusing girls. He pleaded guilty to murder." Moore, who has been in prison for twenty-seven years, has unsuccessfully appeared before a parole board four times. Relin believes the social worker loves Moore purely "out of sympathy."

• • •

When Francine met Charlie, she was smitten by his looks, voice, and presence. "I was thunderstruck. . . . There was something about him that was so compelling. . . . He's a lanky-cowboy sort of looking person with a deep, deep Southern accent. . . . He looks like he ought to be herding cattle on a Wyoming ranch. . . . He looks like those mythical Western figures that you read about."

A professional woman who returned to college in her late thirties, Francine was dedicated to her career as a photographer. But after the day her job sent her into a prison and she ran into her Marlboro Man, love took precedence. "It threw my career so far offtrack, it was unbelievable. . . . I remember him as one of the most attractive people I had ever seen in my life. Nothing I have ever found out has altered that image or changed it in any way. He's over six feet, weighs about one hundred eighty pounds. He has large, luminous, expressive eyes and a very direct gaze; there's something very hopeful in his face."

It was more than physical attraction, though. "I recognized him. . . . I was not meeting someone who was a stranger. . . . I felt an enormous affinity for him." She echoes many other women who have fallen for murderers. It's not just a quickening of the heartstrings and the hormones; their love is a deep feeling, a sense of coming home. "When he and I began to converse, it was as though we had known each other always. . . . The first time that we spoke together . . . I was having a conversation with someone I had known all my life." Of course, Charlie felt the same way. "No one he had ever met in his life had an impact on him like me."

In 1963, he shot and killed a store clerk during a robbery. He was twenty. Charlie was convicted of murder in 1963 and sentenced to death.

His death sentence was later reduced to life imprisonment. A determined man who has filed many unsuccessful appeals, Charlie is still in prison despite recommendations by several parole boards that he be released.

Francine admits Charlie killed the store clerk, but she doesn't believe he intended to do it; she also thinks it was a form of self-defense since the clerk was a "big guy" and was coming at Charlie. "He killed the guy. He'll say that and he'll say he should have served a long time. . . . He loaded the gun but he didn't put a bullet in the loading chamber. . . . [The victim] was a big guy. Although [Charlie's] six feet, he was kind of a shrimp of a guy. He wasn't very heavy."

Francine, forty-one and fairly sophisticated when she met Charlie, was aware that convicted murders are usually guilty. "I was not . . . bedazzled by some glamorous outlaw-convict type. This man had been convicted of murder. I gathered . . . all the information I could. I really cared what happened to him, but I didn't want to be a fool." It turned out that Charlie had a record. Francine was shocked. The murder, well, she could get around that. But she could not wish away his lifetime pattern of criminality. "If you're looking at a man who's done a murder and that's the only thing he's done—that's one thing. But if you find out there are all these other convictions, that gives you pause."

But only pause. Swept away by her passion for Charlie, she overlooked his record, his past. "I looked at the number of years he had been in [prison]. . . . He was totally rehabilitated and utterly trustworthy. . . . He had a good prison record. If [he] were a violent person, he certainly would have engaged in violence while in prison [so] that proved he was a changed individual." Most of his crimes were done when he was young, she rationalized, between the ages of seventeen and twenty. And the murder? Well, that was the result of a robbery he got "mixed up in" because of another man. "He had a friend . . . [who] was on the run. . . . That's how [he] got mixed up in this robbery. . . . He had done other holdups, but this is the one in which the guy died. He did six years on death row."

As she became more and more involved with Charlie, Francine decided to leave her husband. Even though she hadn't been in love with him for years—she had certainly never felt about him the way she did about Charlie—they had had children together, had been married for more than a decade. But the loyalty she felt toward her husband dimmed when compared to the bright glow of her intense passion for Charlie. Charlie is "something that happened" to Francine "like a plane falling out of the sky or a train running over me." She believes that true love eliminates free choice. "It was not the kind of love relationship that you say to yourself, 'I'm going to choose to be involved in this' or 'I'm going to choose not to be involved in this.' If you have the ability to do that, then you're not in love with the person. You're not. Because you don't have the depth of emotion or feeling—not if it is like what happened to me."

She fantasized that Charlie would eventually be released. "I never believed that he was going to do natural life." She didn't take into consideration his six years on death row, his sentence of life without parole, or the state he was in with its reputation for being extraordinarily tough on convicted killers.

Lisa Petrocelli, a nurse, first contacted her murderer/husband Tracy through an inmate in the Las Vegas jail where she worked. Married in 1988, Lisa and Tracy want to have a baby. But since Tracy is on death row, prison officials will not allow conjugal visits. Nor, they said, are they planning to develop an artificial insemination program. The Petrocellis are suing the State of Nevada to force officials to allow either conjugal visits or artificial insemination. Tracy, thirty-eight, is in prison for shooting to death a Reno car dealer while on a test drive in 1982. This was not his first murder. He was also sentenced to life in prison for murdering his ex-girlfriend in Seattle in 1981.

Nevada prison spokesman Glen Whorton said Tracy "likes to talk, likes sports . . . is extroverted and outspoken." He described Lisa as "very demure, very introverted and quiet, a person who naturally does have compassion for the sick." Said Lisa: "All Tracy and I have is love and time.

We are running out of time. . . . I want to have this baby, and I do not think God would think it is wrong to bring a new baby into the world."

SCAMS

Convicted killers sometimes run scams on unsuspecting women that revolve around money and/or pornography. One woman was told by the inmate she loved to send $4,000 to an "early-release board" to buy him a pardon. She did, but the money really went to another inmate's sister; then the two inmates divided it between them, according to Paul Decker, assistant warden at Florida State Penitentiary.

"It is one of the scams among con men to try to find a woman. There are a lot of guys in [prison] who go through one woman after another," said Alicia, who loves Bill, a murderer.

Rochelle, married to a murderer, believes many of the women in love with murderers are being duped (but not her, of course). "First is the woman who met him through a mail-order catalog. She's answering an ad and he's sweet-talking her. She's usually bringing in drugs. She's called a mule. Ninety percent of the women are bringing in something. . . . Another type of woman brings in money but not drugs. The inmate says, 'Why don't you just bring me a fifty-dollar bill this week? I can get more in the canteen if I have cash instead of just money on the books.' "

NO REASONABLE EXPLANATION

Then there are the stories that can't be categorized, the free women who meet killers in unique ways. Mary Bain met murderer Joseph Pikul because their daughters attended the same school.

Jennifer Bain and Claudia Pikul were privileged little

girls who attended a private school in Manhattan. Mary, Jennifer's mother, thought that Claudia's Wall Street–analyst father, Joseph, was arrogant and standoffish. "He was a little snobbish and didn't have much to do with anyone. One night we went to the ballet at Lincoln Center and my daughter ran into Claudia. The two girls were squealing with joy over seeing each other, but Joseph sort of whisked his daughter away and they got into a limousine."

Sometime later, Mary and Joseph met under circumstances neither of them could ever have imagined. In late autumn 1987, Joseph was arrested for the murder of his wife, Diane, after her body was found dumped in a drainage ditch on the New York State Thruway. In January, the girls' school held a meeting to deal with the double tragedy: the death of Claudia's mother and her father's arrest for murder. Mary, a clothing designer, was struck not by Joseph's being a suspected killer but by his wit, charm, intelligence—and his considerable wealth. They talked, began to spend time together, and after a short but heady courtship, Mary left her husband (the marriage was already in trouble) to live with Joseph in his time of need. (Jennifer remained with her father.) In July, only months after they met, Mary became the third Mrs. Joseph Pikul. To the skeptics who asked why Mary would wed a man about to be tried for murder, she replied, "I couldn't walk away from love. . . . It's something I had fallen into. . . . I got to know the children. . . . I saw what it was for the first time to be loved and appreciated . . ."

During a September 1988 custody hearing in which Joseph unsuccessfully battled his murdered wife's relatives for custody of his children, Mary told a lawyer that she hadn't planned on falling in love. "Love is a once-in-a-lifetime opportunity. You see something so real you can't walk away from it." Mary sacrificed her marriage, lifestyle, and daughter for Joseph Pikul. "I signed everything over to my husband. I literally walked out of the house with the clothes on my back." She also lost her extended family because her relatives wanted nothing to do with her. By the time Joseph was found guilty of murder, in March 1989, Mary was all alone in the world.

Mary had not fallen for a convicted killer; she believed Joseph was innocent, that he killed Diane because she was trying to stab him, that he would not be found guilty and would remain free. But during the months they lived together, both before and during his trial, Mary made many terrifying discoveries. She found out that Joseph had indeed killed his wife and that her own life was in danger. There were incidents during those months: He chased her through the woods near their house, trying to hit her. He slashed a dress she wore with a knife. He told her he was digging a grave for her. Several times, she was forced to call in the local police for help. Perhaps most terrifying, Joseph showed her videotapes in which he revealed his darkest side: He claimed to be a victim of multiple personalities, some of whom were female, and one of whom had killed Diane.

In July 1989, Mary privately expressed doubts about the relationship she had had with Joseph, although, to the public, she maintained the facade of a loyal and loving widow. "I'm beginning to think I used poor judgment. . . . I'm beginning to hate Joe." A short time after his murder conviction, before he could be sentenced, Joseph Pikul became very ill. He was dying of AIDS. (He died June 2, 1989. Because he died before he could be sentenced, his murder conviction was vacated.)

"Joe is screwing me again," Mary said shortly before his final illness. "Joe is scum. He never told me he was homosexual. I just feel this man has screwed me royally."

Still loyal, though, she added, "I fell in love with somebody. . . . I still don't think I did the wrong thing."

Hilary: A Case of Substitution

"He even looks like my father"

LUCAS

One day in April 1983, Hilary walked through the coronary care unit of a large hospital on the outskirts of Pittsburgh, her white uniform whispering, her rubber-soled shoes quiet. She saw that one of the patients had his ankle chained to his bedpost. She was shocked; she had never seen anything like that. And an armed guard stood next to the comatose man.

"I felt sorry for him. That poor man. He has nobody here. . . . I didn't know what he did. Why is he chained to this bed? What is going on?" Hilary walked past the guard and read the patient's chart: Lucas Milton, heart attack. The patient opened his eyes and Hilary talked to him. Happy with the attention, he asked her to come back. She did, and they spoke regularly during his stay in the hospital. When he was released and asked for her phone number, she was hesitant, though. She had long since found out he was an inmate at the state prison. "I gave him the Dial-A-Prayer number instead of my real number."

A few months later, Lucas was back in the CCU and the nurses there called Hilary to let her know. This time, when he was released, she gave him her real phone number. "The first time, I didn't know if I really wanted to get involved. I thought he was really a nice guy, but I wasn't sure. . . . He was incarcerated and I never had any doings with anything like that."

But this time, Hilary agreed to write, and she and Lucas began to correspond. The first letters were chatty, friendly, but rapidly became more intimate. "I realized that I really liked this guy. Maybe I had been a little harsh. If this situation was reversed, if that was one of my family, would I want someone to turn their back on him?"

Choosing not to communicate with Lucas because he was a prisoner would be just like shutting him out in the cold, she thought. Lucas, thirty-eight, and Hilary, forty-five, had a lot in common; when they read, both chose Stephen King novels, and they both liked the same sitcoms on television.

More important, unlike the men she dated after she divorced her first husband, Hilary thought Lucas was perfect. "When I met Lucas, I just couldn't find anything that he was lacking." The only drawback, of course, was that he was in prison for murder. But that didn't stop Hilary and she fell in love. "Lucas is a gentle person, a sensitive man. . . . He's not afraid to cry. He doesn't come off with this big macho-image type thing. He's not afraid to be a human being."

Six months later, Hilary asked Lucas's lawyer if it would benefit him to be married when he filed his next appeal. Sure, said the lawyer. It would look much better for Lucas if he had a wife, an established residence, and a made-to-order family. Lucas demurred, though. "He told me, I hate like hell to tie you down. I don't want you to sit at home and wait. I don't know how long it'll be before I get out of here."

Hilary said she'd live with him when he got released,

but Lucas was too conventional for that. "Lucas said, 'No, I ain't gonna live with you without a piece of paper between us. I don't go for that stuff.' " He did not approve of flouting respectability by living in sin. He wanted it legal.

Hilary, by now very devoted to this man, decided to stick by him no matter what. If it was better for him to be married, she would marry him. She was also determined to get him freed and promised Lucas, "I am going to get you out of here."

FAIRY TALE

Hilary grew up in a sprawling house filled with humanity: her parents, grandfather, and her father's eleven brothers and sisters. As soon as her teenaged parents married— mother, Grace, sixteen, and father, Bob, nineteen—they had moved into an old, three-story house on the outskirts of Pittsburgh to provide a home for Bob's siblings—five of whom had been living in an orphanage—and his father. His mother was dead.

When Grace was seventeen, Hilary was born. The teen-age mother stayed at home caring for her daughter and some of her young brothers- and sisters-in-law while Bob, his father, and two older brothers worked in a steel mill.

How Grace managed this huge family, thrust on her when she was barely out of childhood herself, is a mystery to Hilary. "I don't have the faintest idea how she did it. She must have had the patience of a saint. . . . I know that she's up in heaven now and she got a star for that one." Hilary remains enthralled with the image of her young, but strong, mother taking care of everyone.

Grace and Bob had taken in his family because Bob was "a very devoted family man." With such a large family, holidays, everyday meals, laundry—just about every part of daily life was a huge undertaking. "I can remember my mother starting at five o'clock in the morning and cooking two complete Thanksgiving dinners. They would set the table and then one group would eat. Then they'd clear up and set it again and a second group would start in."

Hilary was happy. She had no siblings to fight with; her aunts and uncles, all older, acted as her protectors. She was the coddled, much-loved baby of the family, sharing a bedroom with an aunt who was only two years her senior. "It was fun. It felt like they were all my brothers and sisters. We looked out for one another. We all had to share everything."

Discipline in the family revolved around attendance at church and adherence to the Golden Rule, but no one was fanatically religious. If his brothers acted up, Bob "would take the belt to them," but he never raised a hand against his baby, Hilary. Neither did her aunts and uncles hit her. The boys would threaten to put her in the closet if she misbehaved, but overall, "they were very protective of the girls."

Her adolescence was also unmarked by trauma. She was a B student who spent much of her time in roller-skating competitions. She got along with both parents. "Me and my mom talked a lot." Her father, who was his high school valedictorian, had plans for Hilary to further her education—"He wanted me to be a lawyer"—but she showed no interest in school. She wanted to get married.

Hilary idolized her father. "He was a very intelligent, understanding person. . . . I could go to him and say, 'Daddy, I don't know what to do.' We would sit there and have great talks. He would always advise me. . . . We would have long talks about everything, about politics." He never acted angry. "If my father got mad, he'd go outside and sit on the front porch."

Unlike some other neighborhood men, he was not a heavy drinker, but on the rare occasions he did get drunk, he was pleasant. "He would come home and have a beer or two. He might go off to the corner bar . . . with the guys on his day off. On holidays, when he did get a little bit too much [to drink], he'd be funny as hell."

Her parents got along well in a relationship Hilary describes as a fifty-fifty partnership. Bob earned the money and Grace decided how it would be spent. They always saved, even if it was only a dollar a week.

Hilary views her childhood as solid, although lacking in luxuries. "When I look back, I had a damn good childhood. We never had a whole lot of money and I never had designer clothes, but I had the basics. And I had somebody that I could go and talk to."

That was most important. Her father was someone to confide in, to share her troubles with, to advise her. To Hilary's unending regret, she gave that up to marry when she was only seventeen. She would spend the rest of her life looking for someone to listen to her problems—a man to take her father's place.

YOUNG LOVE

When Hilary turned seventeen, graduated from high school, and decided to get married, conveniently there was a boy three blocks away who wanted her. They had known each other for years. "I had stars in my eyes. I wanted my own little vine-covered cottage with the picket fence and the kids. It just didn't work out that way."

Her nineteen-year-old husband, Sid, drank a bit and his parents were alcoholics, but that didn't faze Hilary. She knew she could save Sid from becoming an alcoholic like his parents. "I thought maybe if he had someone to come home to and someone to care about him, maybe it would change him." But that didn't happen.

A few years into the marriage, Sid hit Hilary. He apologized. The second time it was easier for him to hit her, then say he was sorry. The third time it was even easier. "It got to the point when I would see him coming home, I'd try to stay out of his way."

They had four children, three boys and a girl. To Hilary and her children, Sid was a brute who thought nothing of punching his family around. Every night, he would stop at

a bar and get drunk. If Hilary was in bed when he came
home, he'd start a fight. If she was asleep, he'd wake her
up. If he arrived in time for dinner, he'd say, "I ain't eating
this slop." If Hilary was out, he'd harass the children. When
she came home, she'd tell them to "go up to their room, but
sometimes he'd follow them up and beat them. . . . He
never touched the girl though."

For their daughter, he reserved special treatment. No
hitting. Just emotional and psychological abuse. "She would
always analyze everything . . . but he would say to her,
'You're nothing but a faker, you're nothing but a slut.' He
would really pull her down as far as self-esteem. One time
she came home from school and complained of pain in her
lower abdomen. . . . He said she was faking, but she really
did have appendicitis. 'Oh, Queenie,' he said, 'you think
you're the great one but you're nothing but dog shit.' . . . I
think he didn't want a girl."

In addition to beating Hilary, he insulted her whenever
he could. "He was always putting me down: 'You're so ugly.
You're so stupid.' " Her husband's outrages upon her body
and mind also included what Hilary describes as "not so
much rape, as force," sexual attacks during the last years of
the marriage.

Sid was unreasonably jealous and accused Hilary of
being intimate with the paperboy, the mailman, the teenager
across the street. "I was not allowed to talk to anybody. An
old man kissed me on the cheek and I took a beating for
it." She did not work outside her home for the seventeen
years of her hellish marriage. She wanted to go back to school
once but Sid would not allow it. "Then I'd get a taste of
independence and he wouldn't like that. He was a very in-
secure person."

It didn't take long for the reality of Sid's drinking and
violence to kill the fantasies in Hilary's head about a vine-
covered cottage. Nor did she get the calm, cozy family life
of which she had dreamed. She had no one to talk to, no
one to advise or comfort her, either. Her attempt to emulate

10

15

20

her mother and be the nurturing center of a large family had failed. She took care of her children, but the family unit was hardly intact; it suffered from daily doses of Sid's emotional and physical abuse.

The marriage ended in a violent confrontation with Hilary wielding a gun. Sid broke her arm, and after she drove herself to the hospital to get the bone set, she came home and put her children to bed. "I didn't want them to see how badly hurt I was. I didn't want to scare them." Then she went downstairs and cradling Sid's hunting shotgun in her good arm, took up a position on the stairs. She put two shells in the gun and sat waiting for her husband to return home from the bar. When he walked in, she flipped on the light and told him, "You take one step towards me and I'll kill you." She pulled the hammer back and he turned white. He backed away, afraid. The marriage was over.

Later, her thirteen-year-old daughter asked her, "Why didn't you do this earlier?"

SINGLE MOTHER

After the divorce, Hilary worked as a waitress in a fast-food place, then went on to a better restaurant. Years passed. After she put her daughter through nursing school, Hilary decided it was her turn and studied nursing at a community college. She graduated in September 1982 and began work as a nurse. "I always wanted to be a nurse. I like helping people." Later, Hilary went back to school again, earning an associate's degree as a paralegal. "I love to go to school. I love education, and now I have two professions I can fall back on."

She dated after her marriage broke up but decided that "all men were jerks. They were stupid. . . . Every man that I met was lacking something. Either they weren't tall enough or they weren't this or that. . . . I thought all men were idiots so I didn't even date for two years."

MURDER FOR BEER

It was true that the old man had very little, but on the first Saturday in December 1972, three young Pittsburgh men believed they had even less and decided to rob him.

Lucas Milton, then twenty-eight, and two friends, planned a break-in to rclieve the old man of money from his just-cashed social security check. The three younger men followed the old man home to his tiny place in Pittsburgh's Northside after he cashed the $289 check at a neighborhood bar. They listened outside the old man's door and heard him talking about having a lot of money. Then they bashed in his door.

Unfortunately for all involved, the old man habitually talked to himself about possessing large sums of money, but in reality he was a pauper. And no match for the youthful burglars. The third man reportedly waited outside with a getaway car while Lucas Milton and the second man broke into the apartment. When the elderly man refused to reveal where he had hidden his cash, they beat him to death. They ran out with four cans of beer they had taken from the refrigerator, but not before one of the burglars tried to decapitate the old man with a saw.

Eighteen years later, the Pittsburgh assistant district attorney who prosecuted the murder case, J. Alan Johnson, said the old man had been a plasterer. His killers, after trying unsuccessfully to cut his head off, covered his body with plaster and then walked outside, leaving dusty white footprints that eventually led police right to them.

In July 1973, Lucas Milton pleaded guilty to murder in the first degree and attempted robbery. He first watched his accomplice's trial result in a first-degree murder conviction, carrying with it a sentence of life without parole. But pleading guilty didn't help Milton, and he, too, was sentenced to life without parole.

Then he was twenty-eight, single, and a killer. He is now forty-six, married to Hilary, and according to the Commonwealth of Pennsylvania, a killer, still serving his term.

To Hilary, Lucas does not belong in prison. "He's a good man, a very good man, religious . . . not a religious fanatic, but a . . . good-hearted, unselfish person. He'd do anything for anybody. . . . Now he has a heart problem, but he carried a man across the yard who [was ill]." Hilary told Lucas, "You made a mistake, you never had a prior record, nothing. You don't deserve to be in here." Even her family agrees. After her grown children met Lucas, they said, "You gotta get him out of here. He's a hell of a man."

DENIAL

Although Hilary is bothered by the murder, she believes his drunkenness is what caused Lucas to beat the old man to death. The Lucas she knows and loves does not have that capacity for violence. "That's not his makeup. If he was in his right mind, if he hadn't been drinking that night . . . I'm not making excuses for him. I know it was the alcohol that did it."

Lucas had a deprived childhood. Raised in an orphanage, his mother was unmarried and he never knew his father. "He never had people that said, 'I love you,' and meant it. . . . He never had anybody. . . . Lucas was fighting it all himself. He never had somebody say, 'That's wrong.' All he had was somebody who would cuff him back of the head. He told me he never had anybody who cared. I do. I care now. . . . Lucas has been hurt enough. I can't let him get hurt anymore." Hilary must protect Lucas to satisfy her own emotional needs. She is his savior; when his attorney files appeals, Hilary goes before the parole board instead of Lucas. "I'm speaking for him. I'm his voice at that time."

SUICIDE

One cold morning in 1986, Lucas tried to end his life by slicing his wrists with a razor he had managed to conceal in his cell. Although he was already married to Hilary and had her strong love in his corner, he wanted to die. Always understanding, Hilary said she can comprehend why Lucas tried to slit his wrists. "My [Lucas] is very, very sensitive. He is so starved for affection, for love. I asked him why. Didn't you stop to think who you were hurting? He said, 'All I could think of was—I'll never get out of here. I'll never be with you.' . . . He couldn't look ahead at that point."

She blames prison life for Lucas's depression. "It's a tense, stressful situation. There are two thousand men in an institution built for eight hundred ninety-five. You live by bells. . . . Everything is regimented. Lucas has no space to walk, no space, period."

In retrospect, however, Lucas's suicide try was beneficial because he was admitted to a state psychiatric hospital where, for the first time, he began to deal with his alcohol dependency. "That's where he learned about alcoholism. He said, 'I would never stand up in front of a bunch of people and say I'm an alcoholic. Now that I know it's a disease, I can do it.' "

Hilary became a hovering angel of mercy to Lucas then. She visited him at the psychiatric hospital although it was hundreds of miles away. "I felt . . . like I was his mother. Get him on the straight and narrow, like a mom does to a kid. He didn't want to go to the mental hospital, but I told him I'd be there. I went every six weeks. I made it there for his birthday and I made it there for Christmas."

LOVE OR THE BOTTLE

Hilary has told Lucas he has to choose between her and drinking. "Lucas knows how I feel about alcohol. I told him,

'You're either going to take me and what I can offer you—
or the bottle, and you're going to die in this place a lonely
old man.' " Unfortunately, Lucas has had a few setbacks in
his resolution to quit drinking. "I'm not saying he didn't slip.
But he always got right back on it." Lucas must stop drinking
because of his poor health. Planning for his release from
prison, Hilary has already contacted an Alcoholics Anonymous chapter near her house to ask if Lucas could be a
speaker.

Sometimes Hilary wavers. She will admit to being afraid
Lucas might drink again. "I have fears what if he goes
drinking again . . . But there's AA and I have faith in
Lucas."

In the early years of her marriage to Sid, Hilary was
certain she could change *his* patterns of drinking and violence. "But then I realized a leopard does not change his
spots." So what's the difference this time, with Lucas? Hilary
is convinced Lucas wants to change whereas Sid never recognized his alcoholism. "My first husband would never admit
he needed help. . . . Lucas, on the other hand, realizes he
does have a problem and that he can't solve it himself."
Also, for the first time in his life, thanks to Hilary, Lucas
"has something he's never had and something he values—a
family."

Still, Hilary will have a large burden if Lucas is released.
In addition to fears he might start drinking, she will have to
support him because his heart condition precludes his working. "I get kind of scared. He won't be able to work . . . so
it'll all be on me. Will I be able to handle all that?" But
Lucas always has the right words for Hilary when she expresses anxieties. "He told me that we'll handle it. If we
have to eat bread and beans, we'll handle it."

Bread and beans? Right now, while he's in prison, Hilary is supporting Lucas in a relatively comfortable lifestyle.
Although she is in her forties, with little money saved, she
does nothing to provide for her own future. All her money—
and she works sixty hours a week—goes to pay bills, hers
and his. And he has some expensive needs: legal fees for

mounting a new appeal; a new color television set because "cell thieves" broke in and took the one he had.

"I'm the one that buys Lucas his TV, his radio, his clothes, and his goodies from Hickory Farms at Christmas. I'm the one who pays for his phone calls." Hilary puts money on his commissary book so he can purchase small items at the prison store. She has had to do without herself to keep him comfortable. "I've been wanting to get a new washer. . . . But when he calls and says, 'It's so cold and all I have is one blanket'—so what's more important, a blanket for him or a new washing machine?"

THE MOTHER

According to psychiatrist Streamson Chua, M.D., Hilary's great motivator is a need to be like her mother. "She admired her mother, who married young and took care of everyone. She wants people with problems so she can take care of them." Her need to nurture is one reason why Hilary has chosen nursing. When she was dating Sid, she knew he drank, was aware his parents were alcoholics, but married him anyway and took on the burden of trying to change him. After Hilary had children, she had to be constantly vigilant to protect them from Sid's violence. Now, in Lucas, she has satisfied her deepest fantasies of being a total nurturer and caregiver. Lucas, with his physical problems, alcoholism, and murder conviction, fills the bill; Hilary can be Earth Mother and Florence Nightingale to this incredibly needy victim. "The more problems that Lucas has, the better it is for her," said Dr. Chua.

Hilary does not easily express emotions, but she will share her feelings with Lucas when she's depressed. For the most part, though, she is *his* rock and has shouldered his financial, legal, physical, and psychological burdens.

GOOD ADVICE

At the same time that Hilary strives to be like her mother, she is trying to find a man who will fill the remembered image of her father—an image that is no doubt seen through a rosy filter. She wanted a kind, understanding father and describes hers as infinitely patient and willing to listen. But anecdotes she tells about him hardly fit the fairy-tale person she describes.

Early in her marriage, when she and Sid fought, she went home to talk it over with her father. She was only eighteen at the time. Her father had always been willing to advise her, but this was different. "He told my mom to make me a cup of coffee . . . and he said, 'You're welcome here anytime. . . . You can come back here . . . but this is no longer your home. . . . When you have a problem, you have to figure it out and you have to settle it.' "

Incredibly, Hilary is grateful for that advice. "If my father had been the type to say, 'Oh, no, no one's doing that to my baby girl,' I might have become too dependent. . . . I might have said to my husband, 'My dad will take care of you.' . . . I have to thank my parents for me being as independent as I am right now. They're the ones that built my character."

Yes, Dad was right to let Sid keep beating up his baby girl; it made her independent. While her parents were building her character, her husband was destroying her body, ripping apart her confidence and self-esteem. "When I was beaten by my ex-husband, I could have asked for help, and I know my parents would have said, 'Come on home.' But . . . it was my bed and I would handle it."

Actually, she did not tell her parents directly that she was being beaten because they had not wanted her to marry Sid. "I didn't tell my parents. Then it would be, 'I told you so.' I didn't want to admit I made a mistake."

When she was bruised, she would make up excuses. Her parents never really believed she walked into a door or fell down the stairs. Still, they did not intercede. "I think they were just waiting for me to do something. . . . I have a lot of pride. . . . I didn't want to admit that I failed.

"When I pulled a gun on Sid, my father wondered why I didn't do that years ago. My parents' attitude was, 'You knew we were always here, but we didn't want to step over the line.' "

SOMEONE, PLEASE LOOK AT ME

Growing up in such a crowded household, it's likely that Hilary didn't receive as much attention as she needed. She is probably fantasizing when she recalls the warmth and love in the family and when she describes her kind, understanding father. "It's a fantasy that her father sat down and talked to her so gently," said psychiatrist Chua.

But Lucas, locked up, a murderer, sick, alcoholic, with no one on the outside caring much about him—Lucas will pay attention to Hilary. Lucas, as do most other convicted murderers, focuses intensely and solely on his woman. He gives her all the attention she could ever want or need—constant phone calls, emotional letters, close, warm personal visits. As do all the wives and girlfriends of these men, Hilary relishes the attention. As long as Lucas satisfies her need for attention, Hilary is willing to sacrifice enormously.

Anything Lucas asks of her, he gets. "If he would call right now and say, 'I need your right arm,' I'd say, 'You got it.' " Lucas "fulfills my needs. I know that sounds strange. I'm here and he's in a correctional institute. We've been married for seven years and he fulfills my needs! [But] sex is not everything. I could be at my lowest point and he's always there to pick me up." (Hilary and Lucas actually had sexual relations once when a guard at the hospital, after finding out they had never consummated their marriage, left them alone for an hour. Hilary said that "it was wonderful and . . . his attorney is afraid that when he gets him out of there, I'm gonna kill him the first night.")

DADDY'S GIRL

While Hilary can recreate her mother's role in the family by providing Lucas with care, stability, security, nurturing, he can be the father she imagined, the man whose memory she embellished out of her deepest needs. When Lucas is released—Hilary is certain it will be soon because he has served seventeen years and has serious health problems—he will "round out the family circle."

"I know he has a lot of my father's qualities. The strange part of it is, he even looks like my father."

Lucas is Hilary's fantasy come to life; if that's love, then she loves him. "There isn't anything I wouldn't do for him and he feels the same way. He's told me many times he would lay down his life for me. There is no other man on the face of this earth that could come up to my Lucas. I have never cared about anybody as much as I care for him."

For more than a decade, Hilary has lived without an abusive, alcoholic man in her house. Perhaps it's time to take up residence with such a man again. Once, when Hilary teased Lucas and told him she had to leave early from a prison visit because she had a date, he said, "Oh, yeah, you want me to knock you out right here?"

No. Hilary will wait until he can knock her out right in her own living room.

Why Women Love Killers

"We're not who you think we are"

We've met several women in love with murderers and found out how they meet their men. In order to understand them, it's necessary to examine their love, to put romance under a microscope and try to comprehend what makes a woman fall in love with a killer.

Through the vagaries of social change, from the Me Generation of the seventies to the New Agers of the eighties, the yearning for romantic love remains central. Love makes the world go round but comes in many shapes—from the perverse to the practical. Romantic love consumes us as we see from television, books, movies, and popular music. With today's waning of the values of the traditional family—because of physical relocation, a 50-percent divorce rate, and other, positive factors such as a decrease in sexual stereotypes—we have seen an increased importance placed on romance, especially for women.

"Passions are the great moving forces in people's lives," said Ethel Spector Person, Ph.D., author of *Dreams of Love and Fateful Encounters: The Power of Romantic Passion.* A fundamental need for romantic love motivates people to act, to seek, to relate. "When you fall in love and you really bridge that chasm and you almost merge with somebody else, there is ultimately a strength, an enlargement, and an enrichment that comes out of it."

Romance is used to sell women on almost every single product, from cars to food. Romantic love makes the world turn on soap operas and in romance novels, two hugely popular and profitable forms of entertainment that have almost half of America mesmerized—the female half. In the world of the soaps, shows that attract millions of devoted viewers, romantic relationships are all turmoil, turbulence, conflict. Best-selling romance novels reach an estimated 20 million people, most of them women.

In recent years, academics have taken up a serious study of the psychology of love. "Romantic love . . . has supplanted religion as the arena in which men and women seek meaning, transcendence, wholeness and ecstasy," writes psychologist Robert A. Johnson, a Jungian analyst, in *We: Understanding the Psychology of Romantic Love.*

Many women use love relationships as an arena for excitement and drama. Although this has slowly been changing due to the influence of the feminist movement, it is still evident, from talking to women in love with murderers, that many women use love as a substitute for other types of excitement. Instead of being aggressive in business or sports, for instance, some women find excitement by falling in love with the wrong men. Many women think they can get satisfaction only from a man: the larger-than-life man . . . the remote man . . . the crazy man . . . the risk-taker . . . the rich and powerful man . . . the macho man. Women who fall in love with murderers display an extreme need to find excitement, satisfaction, fulfillment, from a socially unacceptable man.

These women also have an idealized and romanticized perception that love between man and woman is based on constant passion, unsatisfied yearnings, and ungratified desires. These women search for and find this type of romantic love with eagerness and intensity. Unlike other seekers after romantic love, women who love killers *always* find their Holy Grail. They find it in unlikely places, with unlikely partners. *But they find men to love who will provide them with constant, renewable, unending passion, with undying love—with romance that resembles a soap opera or a romance novel more than it resembles real life.*

By choosing as their lovers men behind bars for committing murder, they have found a way to keep romance, passion, and love alive forever.

How? First, let's look closely at romantic love; then we'll see how women who love killers, how women who marry murderers, are really very successful at what we call "love." They are able to fly around the flame without getting burned to death—maybe only a little singed.

COURTLY LOVE

What is romantic love? Is it something we should search for? Is it good for us? Or is it, as Robert Johnson believes, merely the mask that spirituality wears today?

For women in love with murderers, romantic love *is* spiritual transcendence. They experience an exalted emotion, an ecstatic, transformational love. They soar above the earth and its mundanity, escaping from the trivia and pain— and the reality—of daily life.

Their idea of romantic love is based, although they don't know it, on the medieval concept of courtly love, which downplayed marriage and sexual encounters between knights and their ladies in favor of endless courtship. Women who love killers are also not allowed to experience (normal) marriages or (normal) sexual encounters with the men they love. Johnson explains three characteristics of courtly love that could also be used to describe the relationships between convicted killers and the women who love them.

NO SEX

Courtly love forbade sex because it "was an idealized, spiritualized relationship, designed to lift the [participants] above the level of physical grossness," writes Johnson. Women in love with murderers don't have sex either. All the women who spoke to me expressed revulsion at sex in public visiting rooms.

Although some had a stolen sexual encounter or two at one time or another, all of them downplayed sex. To these women, sex is simply not as important as romance.

Many of the women talked about the intimacy they share with the men even though there is no sex; some said their relationships are successful because there is no sex involved.

"I am as important to him as he is to me," said Dolores. That she and her boyfriend, Louis, who killed a businessman during a robbery twenty-one years ago, have never had sex is an integral part of their relationship. "He has never been able to establish such a long-term relationship with anybody without having sex confuse the whole thing."

After a long friendship, they fell in love, and using the language of courtly love, Dolores describes how Louis changed as he opened up to her. He is "like a flower that's a bud and you can see it opening before your eyes. Maybe that's what I've fallen in love with: this transformation." Dolores, responsible for the transformation of another human being who loves her enough to flower, is made to feel special.

Alicia loves Bill, in prison for life for stabbing a man in 1981 with a butcher knife. Happy to do without sex, she said that romance without sex "is easier for me. . . . I played out my youth as hard as I could till I was sick to death of it." She will most likely never be able to have sex with the man she loves, but that's okay. "I'm not interested in transient sexual relationships. And as long as I'm committed to this relationship, I know I won't be interested in having sex on the side."

They will never sneak into the little room outside the visitors' room that some couples bribe the guards into letting them use. It's just not worth it. "If there's no chance of getting caught and it's very private and the chance comes up, we'll take it. But if it's going to endanger his case in any way, no."

Elena loved Terry so much she married him despite the many obstacles: her grown children who resented their mother's having a husband in their age bracket; the state that wanted to execute Terry; the fact they could never be alone in a room together because he was a death-row inmate.

"We couldn't live together, but other than that, it was just perfect." Their "chemistry was perfect" but they couldn't *do* anything about it. "We talked about ideas. Sex was something we skirted around because we couldn't have it. . . . He was not a grabby kind of man." A few days before Terry's execution, a sympathetic guard put the very-much-in-love married couple alone in a room together. But nothing happened. "That might have been an opportunity but he was not that kind of man. He would not have grabbed me and done something with the chance a guard would come in. . . . He was very respectful of me as I was of him. Just that act wasn't that important to us. You can get that on the street."

NO MARRIAGE

Courtly love precludes marriage between the knight and his lady. Although many women in love with murderers who are behind bars marry the men, their relationships are hardly intimate; they can't relate as normal husbands and wives. Even those women who try to make their marriages as normal as possible fail dismally. Marriage and intimacy do not flourish under prison conditions. Marrying a man sentenced to life in prison is taking on a situation with guaranteed separation and loss. It means choosing to have a relationship that exists in an artificial, repressive, and threatening environment.

ONLY PASSION

By not allowing sex, marriage, or intimacy, the focus of courtly love becomes, solely, passion. Writes Johnson: "The courtly lovers keep themselves aflame with passion . . . they suffer intense desire for each other, yet strive to spiritualize their desire . . . *by never reducing their passion to the ordinariness of sex and marriage."* (Emphasis added.)

This is the incredible nature of the love between women on the outside and convicted killers. These women have found a way to keep themselves aflame with passion. By choosing as her beloved a man who has committed murder, a man who will never be able to be a regular husband or lover, each woman keeps her passion burning by endless, painful, limitless suffering.

Women who love murderers "are a real romantic breed. They have to be to put up with what they put up with. . . . Their relationships become very dramatic. . . . The Department of Corrections constantly does these horrible things and [the man and the woman] feel defenseless and they get very romantic," said Alicia.

These women don't choose their relationships; they just "fall" madly in love. They are victims of love with no control over their feelings. "I don't think you make the choice to pursue it. It ends up unfolding in front of you and you move with it," said Mary.

"Bill is just—I don't know—it was one of those things. . . . I think I was swept off my feet the first time I heard his voice on the phone. . . . I just love his voice, it's the sexiest voice ever. He's got this deep, heavy Southern accent," said Alicia.

Kay, with a history of unsuccessful relationships, fell desperately and instantly in love with a man serving a life sentence for murder because her first glimpse of him rendered her helpless with swooning passion: "Oh, my God, he is fine. . . . I didn't even know who I was. What is this man doing in here? He was so handsome. He looked like a black messiah, a black Jesus Christ. He had these big, black, piercing eyes and a wonderful voice."

Elena, recalling the love she had for Terry, said, "I loved him. I absolutely adored him. . . . I loved him beyond sanity, probably." Imagine the ecstasy of her suffering as he was taken away to be executed! The passion, the pain! Will she ever again feel as deeply? "His family was clutching at him and crying, and he turned around to me and he looked straight into my eyes and he said, 'You, I love.' And they shackled him and took him away." Those words, that moment, will sustain her for the rest of her life.

There are no bounds to this romantic love, no limits to its depth—or to the pain these women suffer. One notorious woman who loved a murderer—and suffered great losses because of her love—was Tennessee attorney Mary Pentecost Evans. Her lover, William Timothy Kirk, described by another woman married to a murderer as "quite the cavalier and the gentlemen," was originally a client. Kirk, charged with being the triggerman during a prison uprising in which seven white inmates took four guards hostage and killed two black inmates, was to be represented by the court-appointed Evans on the murder charge.

They met in the attorneys' room at Brushy Mountain Prison in Tennessee. He was a career criminal who ran with a rough crowd. Already serving a life sentence for armed robbery and other felonies when he was brought up on this new charge, murder, there was little hope that Kirk, thirty-six, would ever get out of prison. Mary Evans was blond, beautiful, bright, from a wealthy family. Both Kirk and

Evans, twenty-six, had been married and divorced before. But the day they met, it was as if no one else in the world had ever existed.

Evans arranged for Kirk to be transported from prison to a psychologist's office on March 31, 1983, supposedly for a routine consultation. But the couple, by now crazy in love, had planned a daring escape. Evans gave Kirk a gun, and he disarmed the three guards who had accompanied them to the psychologist's office. The pair ran out to her car and drove off. They were on the road for more than four months before they were captured in a motel in Daytona Beach, Florida.

There was a lot of talk in Knoxville about what made Mary Evans do it. No one could understand the appeal Kirk had for her. No one, to this day, ever has. But theories abounded. Evans's boss, Knoxville lawyer James A. H. Bell, was quoted in *The Knoxville News-Sentinel* as saying that Evans may have become "psychologically hypnotized" by Kirk. He even suggested Evans was suffering from the Stockholm Syndrome, a deep emotional bond that can develop between hostage and captor, implying that Kirk had kidnapped Evans. (In 1973, a Swedish woman became so emotionally involved with a bank robber who held her hostage that she fell in love with him, broke her engagement to another man, and remained committed to the bank robber during his trial and subsequent incarceration.)

The psychologist in whose office the daring escape took place speculated that Evans simply loved Kirk. "What I think happened is that she fell in love with him. . . . It is hard for a man in prison to brainwash his lawyer. I think you have to consider the male-female aspect of this thing," said Dr. Gary Salk, quoted in *The Knoxville News-Sentinel*.

"Yeah, she was beautiful. . . . It wasn't like she was some ugly lawyer who was man hungry. . . . It was unusual that she would suddenly fall in love with a killer," said Robert Fellman, a staff attorney for the Tennessee State Board of Professional Responsibility.

Evans's defense during her trial for aggravated kidnap-

ping, armed robbery, and escape was that she was temporarily insane. If *temporary insanity* is a euphemism for mad,
passionate love, then her defense was valid. While she and
Kirk awaited trial, they kept in touch through their lawyers
and by telephone. "I think that's obvious," answered Kirk's
lawyer, Steve Oberman, when asked if the couple was still
in love.

Evans was tried, convicted, and disbarred; she served
two years in jail and moved to Florida, where she has reportedly married. Kirk is in prison; his earliest parole-
consideration date is 2013.

But there is an incredible footnote to this story. Only
one year after this shocking romance and escape, Kirk manipulated another woman into falling in love with him. Her
name also is Mary. They married in 1985 and two years later
had a son. Kirk sees his wife twice a week and they communicate daily by telephone, he told Geraldo Rivera on a
television show that aired August 26, 1988. "We deal with
the same problems and situations on a daily basis that any
other husband and wife do, I imagine."

Rivera asked Mary if she worried that her husband was
exploiting her. "Is he using you so that the parole board
might hear his plea for clemency or for lenient treatment?
Is he using you and this boy?" Mary said she had wanted to
marry Kirk and have his child. "I had the choice. He didn't
make the choice for me. . . . I'm not fascinated by him because he's done crimes or because he's in prison. I met him
when he was on escape."

Is it possible that Kirk had two women in love with him
when he escaped—Mary, his then-lawyer, and Mary, his
now-wife?

Another woman on the same program, Deborah Lee,
told Rivera that her fiancé is serving a 150-year term. Her
passion for him led her to divorce her husband, a Baptist
minister. She initially tried to resist loving her murderer,
said Lee, but passion overpowered her. "I tried not to. I
fought it. But my heart . . . I knew that I was doing

something that morally was wrong, and I tried to back out of it. . . . I just couldn't do it. I loved him so I kept going."

COMPANIONSHIP

The romantic passion experienced by women who love convicted killers never, ever becomes ordinary, everyday love, what some call companionship or companionate love. This affectionate bonding is a warm, tender sharing based on the exchanges of a mutual daily life together. But the special population of women in this book who have fallen in love with murderers has found a way to stave off this more relaxed kind of love. After these women fall in love, they maintain a high level of intensity with their murderer/lover; the relationship does not change into companionate love. It remains eternally romantic.

But some psychologists and psychiatrists give no credibility to romantic love, saying our culture creates an addictive attitude toward love. If the measure of love is its destructiveness to the two lovers and their families, it's not healthy. These experts advise against a romantic love that brings suffering, suggesting instead a down-to-earth, painless love that brings comfort and companionship.

Only "consummate love" is real love, writes psychologist Robert Sternberg in his essay "The Psychology of Love" in a book of the same name. Consummate love has three aspects: intimacy, passion, and decision/commitment. Passionate love is "a continual interplay between elation and despair, thrill and terror, positives and negatives," agrees psychologist Elaine Hatfield in her essay "Passionate and Companionate Love" from *The Psychology of Love*. Hatfield contrasts the radical ups and downs of passionate or romantic love with companionate love. According to her, *companionate love is characterized by more positives than by negatives* and by an exchange of affection in a loving relationship where partners are capable of both intimacy and independence.

Women who fall in love with convicted killers don't want the companionate love described by Hatfield or the consummate love described by Sternberg. These women urgently seek a love that causes discomfort and pain because they want to ride the crests of the waves, lingering over the highs and lows, suffering intensely, denying themselves the normalcy of an average, everyday kind of relationship. These women want passion and won't take anything less. And they accept that passion means suffering. (According to the *Oxford English Dictionary*, compact edition, 1971, the root of the word *passion* means "to suffer"—the sufferings of pain, the sufferings of Christ on the cross.)

An excellent example is the story of Kate Soffel, told by Ron Nyswaner, author of an original screenplay for the movie *Mrs. Soffel*. In 1900, Kate Soffel was the wife of the warden of Pittsburgh's Allegheny County Prison and mother of their four children. A year later, she was in prison, having fallen passionately in love with one of her husband's charges. Her obsessive love for Ed Biddle, a murderer and robber who was sentenced to death, was so overpowering that Kate threw away everything she had to be with him. She helped him and his brother escape from prison and fled with them on New Year's Day, 1901. At some point during their crazed one-day run for freedom, Kate and Ed realized they would be captured. Kate's passion for Ed was such that she could not live without him so she asked him to shoot her; she preferred dying to going back to her regular life. He shot her, but the bullet missed its mark and she lived. Ed was killed when the runaways were captured.

Kate, in her early thirties, first met Ed when she read the Bible to him. That, as well as supervising food preparation and making sure the inmates had blankets, were her responsibilities as warden's wife. Ed, twenty-four, and his brother were doomed to die and had become a *cause célèbre*, capturing the imaginations of the women of Pittsburgh. Ed, in particular, was handsome, smart, eloquent, and genuinely poetic. Women stood outside the prison every day, praying for the brothers, protesting their imprisonment and their imminent hanging.

After the brothers were killed during their escape attempt, their funeral turned out to be one of Pittsburgh's most well-attended events. Hundreds of grief-stricken women sobbed over the brothers. Because of her sorrow over Ed's death, one teenaged girl committed suicide by ingesting lye. Like Kate Soffel and the women of Pittsburgh, she had fallen under Ed's spell.

Kate, who had encountered passion for the first time in her life when she fell in love with Ed, was never to know it again. She would, however, know a different kind of suffering. After her capture, she served two years in prison. Her husband did not allow her to see their children, and she died five years after her release. She had nothing to live for.

Companionate love is the kind of love that allows lovers to see each other's faults and flaws, weaknesses and needs. It is love that flourishes on commitment and reason, not on wild upswings of irrational expectations, on mad passion, on ecstatic joinings and despairing partings. It is not the love experienced by women who love convicted killers.

FALLING IN LOVE

Women who love murderers, like everyone else looking for love, are seeking transcendence, elevation above the daily routines of life, completion, a feeling of being totally united with another so the self can never again feel the awfulness of existential loneliness. This falling in love, to most of these women, means losing control over their emotions, being totally consumed by an obsession that takes precedence over everything else in their lives.

• • •

Carla, whose husband is currently on Florida's death row after his conviction for the beating and stabbing murder of an elderly woman when he was sixteen, described her passion: "I have never been in love. I had many boyfriends, but now I know I'm in love. . . . I will love him no matter where he is. My feelings will not change."

Mary loves Al, a convicted killer, very much; her feelings for him are deep, passionate, and committed. She talked about the sacrifice that is a necessary part of her relationship: "This is a burning question inside every woman—What is the extent of my love? Could I ever love like that? Are they crazy? Would I be crazy to do that?"

Falling in love is "prompted by an internal psychological state," said Dr. Ethel Person. H. G. Wells wrote of "the Lover Shadow," an explanation for love at first sight. If a woman sees someone and instantly loves him, it's likely he fits her image of her lover shadow. The lover shadow "is made up of many, many different things—memories, sensations, wishful fantasies," said Dr. Person. And that's okay, she added, unless a person "can only fall in love with somebody who is a disaster." Like a murderer.

Women who love killers are seeking the oblivion of total passion, total commitment, total giving up of the self to another. Does it sound religious or spiritual? It is. When we love, "we believe we have found the ultimate meaning of life, revealed in another human being," writes Robert Johnson. Searching for the meaning of life in another person is part of romantic love. And passion is the fuel. Not sexual passion, but the passion of transcendence, ecstasy, intensity, extremes of joy and despair.

Women who love murderers experience all this: They suffer deeply. Their love flourishes in an atmosphere that tries to kill it. For women who love killers, every prison visit presents an opportunity for a tearful, joyous reunion, a demonstration of intense feelings and a sharing of devotion.

Every parting is an opportunity for tears of despair, cries of eternal love, and feelings of longing. *A single prison visit contains as much drama and intensity as a romance novel or soap opera.* The women relish these incredible highs and lows; they live for them and on them.

DRAMA

"One of the great paradoxes in romantic love is that it never produces human relationship as long as it stays romantic. It produces drama, daring adventures, wondrous, intense love scenes, jealousies and betrayals," writes Johnson. Women who love men who kill are *always* in a romantic relationship. They experience continuous excitement and tension: Will the prison let me in? How much time will we have together? What's happening with his appeal? Will he get out? Will he spend the rest of his life behind bars?

In addition to the adventure of their prison visit together, there is the great drama of his life behind bars, as well as her life on the outside. Each week, they exchange impassioned stories. He was attacked by an inmate with a knife. A guard harassed him. He was found with a newspaper in his cell and punished with four days in the hole. She was insulted on the telephone by her parents for having this relationship. She could only work a regular forty-hour week so she can't buy him new shoes this week. And so on.

ILLUSION

Romantic love can be an emotion felt by one person and directed at another—a feeling that considers the happiness and well-being of the beloved as most important. Or romantic love can be an illusion, a reflection of the lover's own desires and fantasies. "Hence the popular idiom that love is blind, for a lover projects onto a partner, or love-blot, his/her unique love image," writes John Money, Ph.D., in *Love and Lovesickness: The Science of Sex, Gender Differences and Pairbonding.*

Women in love with killers refuse to see faults in their men. And they bestow upon their inappropriate partners qualities that most objective observers can see are not real.

These women do not allow themselves to admit their men have weaknesses. They deny the murders their lovers have committed. Their love is fed on illusion and fueled by fantasy so they naturally have false beliefs about the natures of the men they love.

These women love a shadow lover of their own creation. It's as if each woman has taken a blank canvas and painted her ideal man, then fallen in love with him, making him come to life in the process. He is an ink blot, a blank, a reflection of her inner needs; he, and the love she feels, are not real.

THE MEN THEY LOVE: HEROES AND KNIGHTS

The murderers these women love are similar to the heroes of popular romance novels. Readers devour the heroes in the books because, in real life, no men like these ever cross their doorsteps. These heroes are long, lean, and mean— but also loving, caring, and giving to the women who win their hearts. There is no doubt the men are hot-tempered and capable of violence and passion; they've proven that by murdering. But they are also tender. Rochelle's husband is "sensitive to the tiniest of animals" although he is convicted of rape, kidnapping, and murder. Over and over these women describe the men they love as caring, thoughtful, concerned human beings.

According to their women, these men are one-of-a-kind guys. They are leaders, bright, articulate, handsome. Bill "is intelligent, politically, philosophically. . . . He's very liberal. He's very positive; he's one of those power-of-positive-thinking people," said Alicia. Bill is also smarter than she is: "He's a whiz at computers and math. His areas of knowledge are more than mine."

Naomi Zack, a Ph.D. in philosophy, in her introduction to *My Return*, written together with her murderer/husband, Jack Henry Abbot describes him as "one of the most promising young philosophers" of her generation. (In 1981, Abbott stabbed Richard Adan to death.) Abbott is so brilliant, even Zack can't understand some of his writing. To her, he is a genius, an existential hero, and finally, a tragic figure. Writes Zack: "He has paid—more than any man today who has been convicted of manslaughter—for the events of that fateful night—both in the time he has so far served and in his dangerous circumstances in prison."

But there is a more tragic figure: Richard Adan. In her obsessive and delusional love for Abbott, Naomi Zack has forgotten the real victim.

MASTERY AND CHALLENGE

Murderers are also masterful, like romance-novel heroes. Very often, even though they are imprisoned, they are consulted by their girlfriends or wives on life issues. Generally, to his woman, the word of her man is law *even though he is a powerless inmate behind bars.* Bill has a dominating personality, admits Alicia, and he tries to control her. But her denial mechanism clicks in quickly and she softens this statement. "He has a dominating personality but only in the sense that he's very cocky and intelligent and he simply likes to be right. He has a tendency to think he knows a little bit more about most subjects. . . . And he's right. He does know more than most of the people around him."

Consulting a prison inmate is a sham, because if a man is in for murder, he has little control over anything. It is the woman's *need* to see her man as masterful that makes her ask him what she should do and causes her to seek his control and advice.

"One of a woman's most pervasive fantasies is being

Swept Away by the man of her dreams," writes Carol Cassell in her book, *Swept Away*. Although no woman interviewed for this book chose to fall for a murderer, they each described sensations of being swept away by the uncontrollable fervor of their love.

Each woman fantasizes that her man is a hero, a knight in shining armor, so he can save and protect her—not only from the world but from himself and the threat of his own violence. Every man is special and none is a con who uses women. "In [my man's] case, he's not much of a con man. I think our relationship is somewhat different," said Alicia.

Each woman in love with a killer views her man as her salvation: He will save her from loneliness, from selling herself in the meat market of singles bars where rejection is always a threat, from the potential sexual threat of other men. And by making him into a knight, a hero, the woman dilutes what is perhaps the greatest threat of all: that he murdered once and if he had the chance, might just murder again and she might be the victim. After all, her subconscious reasons, Sir Lancelot would never hurt a damsel in distress or force himself on her.

Many of these women are drawn to their murderer/lover because the men represent challenges; relationships with them are obstacle courses. Meeting him, earning his love, making the relationship work despite the tremendous odds against it—women who love killers thrive on these challenges.

Also, these men are "bad," socially unacceptable, extremely macho, because they have killed. If a man is certified masculine, then a woman can be more sure of her femininity; with a man whose maleness or machismo is exaggerated, a woman feels most womanly. These "bad" boys, these killers, fulfill some part of the woman's desire for excitement, for challenge, for adventure—and even make her feel more of a woman. "Crime holds a special attraction for middle class women, who don't turn to it out of economic hardship or peer pressure," writes Joy Davidson, Ph.D., in *The Agony of It All*.

• • •

Who are the women whose psychological needs impel them to seek this type of intensity in their love relationships? Which women must have romantic love that never ends—an unchanging courtship, filled with agony and ecstasy? Why do they want the illusion of romance rather than real love?

These women are satisfied with a love relationship that exists under conditions the majority of us would avoid and find awful. In *Women Who Love Too Much,* Robin Norwood writes: "Prison wives . . . represent perhaps the ultimate example of women who love too much. Because they are incapable of any degree of intimacy with a man, they choose instead to live with a fantasy, a dream of how much they will love and be loved someday when their partner changes and becomes available to them. But they can be intimate only in fantasy."

We must keep in mind the difference between "prison wives," "women who love too much," women who are addicted to love relationships—and women who love murderers. Murderers are special. Women who love murderers are special, also, although they share some characteristics and qualities with women addicted to love relationships/women who love too much. Murderers have acted with total disregard for societal mores. They have shed someone else's blood. The women who love them accept this as part—perhaps the most alluring part—of them. Murderers and their women, who can't live without each other but are forced to remain apart, may be under the spell of *"death love"*—the German concept of *Liebestod.* By worshiping death—or the men who have caused death—these women find the union they cannot find in life. Death becomes the orgasm, the high, the kick.

Denial

"He never meant for this to happen"

Women who love killers don't really *love* at all. They *need*. They *fantasize*. But what they feel for men who kill can hardly be described as love. These women are totally deluded about the men they think they love—"practically living in a trance state," said Charlotte Kasl, Ph.D., author of *Women, Sex and Addiction*. "Each woman totally colludes with her man's denial system. She is absorbed into his being. She and he are enmeshed into one person. They bond through this incredible denial," said Kasl. "There is no human connection."

Al committed a murder—but not really. It was during the robbery of a tiny store in a run-down section of Boston. "He was shot in the back and was knocked into the door. His gun discharged and he killed somebody who was standing in the wrong place." The store owner, who was armed with a shotgun, shot Al first, causing Al's gun to discharge. Result: one dead store clerk.

The store wasn't a respectable shop; it was a front for a bookie joint. Anyway, Al was manipulated into committing the robbery by junkie friends. "His friends took him along on a stickup. . . . He was given a gun." Al was just a nice guy standing there in the middle of a robbery holding a gun that someone had shoved in his hand. And passive, he did not shoot his gun; it went off. "The store owner had been standing in the loft surrounded by an arsenal, with a loaded weapon." This Rambo-type store owner defending his business was guilty of overkill: He had too many weapons and was too quick to shoot the burglars. "[Al] had a semiautomatic in his hand and it discharged, killing a woman clerk. He was standing six feet from her; it hit her in the chest. . . . He never meant for this to happen. If he didn't intend this, then he can't really be guilty."

This version of the murder committed by Al is told by his wife, Mary, who must deny his guilt to be able to continue loving him. She does not want to accept that he armed himself, went into a store to commit a robbery, and then, probably in a moment of panic, killed a clerk. Her denial mechanism is stronger than her rational, clearheaded socialworker side.

What I never heard from any woman interviewed was a simple statement: Yes, the man I love committed a murder, but I have forgiven him and love him anyway. Each woman excused her lover's murder; some concocted fabulous rationalizations to explain how the murder took place. These rationalizations range from the fantastically intricate to the simple. Some women create unbelievably involved denials (see the next chapter). Others excuse the murder by blaming it on social forces or drugs and alcohol. These denials are part of each woman's individual defense mechanism for coping.

If a woman falls in love with a murderer, she must attribute his behavior to something—either to psychological causes or to outside factors—in order to exonerate him. She can't admit he's a murderer *inside,* that he has the heart and soul of a killer. Otherwise, *she* would be crazy for loving him.

"She denies the true character of the man regardless of whether he will [later] abuse her or murder someone else," said psychologist Stuart Fischoff, Ph.D. She compartmentalizes the fact that he has murdered, taking it out of the context of his personality. Then she can deny the murder's importance.

Here are some examples of denials in which each woman describes her view of the murder committed by the man she loves:

- He meant to shoot over her head.
- He was framed.
- He shot in self-defense because the man was coming at him.
- He was drunk.
- He was stoned.
- My husband is serving a ninety-nine-year sentence for murder. . . . He swears to me he is not guilty.
- He didn't mean to kill; it was unintentional.
- There are degrees of the reprehensibility of these crimes.
- They've got the wrong man in prison.
- My husband was guilty with mitigating circumstances.

While it's true that a large number of convicted murderers had terrible childhoods, the women who love them emphasize the detrimental effects of these childhoods. But they always add a disclaimer: "I'm not trying to excuse his behavior." Carla married Martin, a Florida death-row inmate, in 1989, more than a decade after he bludgeoned an elderly woman to death. He was sixteen at the time. "He

was chronically sniffing gasoline for four or five years. . . .
He had a history of being sexually abused by his uncle and
cousin. His father, an alcoholic, used to punch his mother
around. They'd catch him sniffing gasoline and they'd whip
him," said Carla. She describes the murder, using the psychological jargon she's picked up as the wife of a death-row
inmate, as an "isolated explosive disorder."

Despite Martin's dysfunctional family—and despite the
fact that in four separate trials, he was convicted of murder
and sentenced to die—Martin is "a great person. You'd
never think he had that childhood. . . . He's a very nice guy.
He cares about what happens to people," according to his
wife. She sounds as if she's describing a totally different man,
not the Martin who has been convicted four times, who
struck an elderly woman with a glass vase and wrench, then
dragged her into the kitchen where he stabbed her sixty-
seven times with a kitchen knife and sexually abused her
with his fist. Carla also denies that Martin will die: "You
have to kind of pray for the best. . . . If he's sentenced to
die—I just don't believe that's going to happen this time,"
she said before his fourth conviction.

Ruben "is a beautiful person, inside and out." He was
sentenced to twenty years to life for a murder committed
during an armed robbery—felony murder—so he did not
actually kill anyone. "The only reason he got caught was he
got shot and he couldn't get away." Why was he committing
a robbery in the first place? "He was with other people,"
said Kay, the woman who loves him.

Several years after his execution for a double homicide,
Terry's crime is still not something his widow, Elena, can
talk about. On a segment of the Geraldo Rivera television
talk show, "The Wives of Death Row," Elena said the murder Terry committed "was thirty seconds of his
life. . . . That's not all the man was." She added, "I would
really prefer not to go into his crime. No murder is pretty.

I don't justify any murder. I don't justify what he did as right. . . . Although there were circumstances."

With women who love men who kill, there is always *although*. There are always circumstances. There are always excuses. There are, mostly, denials.

In an interview broadcast on the Fox 5 television network, Shawn Kovell discussed her love for Robert Chambers, a love undiminished by knowing he had killed Jennifer Levin—perhaps a love enhanced by that knowledge. "He's a special person. . . . He's caring. He's warm. He's funny. . . . I know it [was] an accident. . . . He's not that type of person. I know him well. I've been with him long enough . . . that he would never intentionally hurt anyone for any reason."

Only six weeks before he killed Richard Adan, Jack Henry Abbott was paroled from Marion Federal Prison in Illinois. He had spent most of his life in institutions—foster homes, then a reformatory, then prison—a life of torment as he described it in his 1982 book, *In the Belly of the Beast*. When the book was published, Abbott, then thirty-seven, was hailed as a brilliant writer by Norman Mailer and other members of the literary establishment. Mailer helped convince a parole board that Abbott could earn his living by his pen. A short time later, Abbott, who had never lived outside the walls of an institution, was sent to a halfway house in New York City.

Weeks later, during a dispute in a restaurant on the Lower East Side, Abbott stabbed to death an out-of-work actor working as a waiter, Richard Adan. Abbott ran and eluded police for a few months. When he was caught, he was convicted of murder and sentenced to a New York State prison where he will likely spend the rest of his life. In *In the Belly of the Beast*, which is dedicated to Carl Panzram, a notorious serial killer, Abbott demonstrates his romanticizing of criminals and violence. "It is the high esteem we naturally have for violence, force. It is what makes us effective, men whose judgment impinges on others, on the world. Dangerous killers who act alone and without emotion . . . this is a state-raised convict's conception of manhood in the highest sense," writes Abbott. But Colin Wilson, in *A Criminal History of Mankind,* writes that murdering Richard Adan was an act of cowardice, not heroism, "about as heroic as strangling a baby."

Abbott has written that he acted violently in a violent world, that he had no choice but to kill when it was necessary to kill. Two years after he murdered Adan, Abbott met Naomi Zack, a resident of a small upstate New York town and a Ph.D. in philosophy from Columbia University. To Zack, according to one friend of hers, Abbott is an existential hero who allows nothing but purity to guide his actions, actions that are truer, more honest, and more valid than most people's.

Five years after Abbott's murder conviction, Abbott and Zack, by then deeply in love, collaborated on *My Return,* Abbott's apologia for the murder of Adan. And Zack's cry of denial.

The introduction to the book, written by Zack, is replete with denials: "The incident was something ordinary, but everyone refused to understand it. . . . What happened was simply this: The man [Abbott] was returning from an after-hours club. . . . The man had a disagreement with the night manager [Adan]. The night manager finally drew a knife to intimidate him, and the man stabbed the night manager one time and killed him accidentally. . . . No one admits that the night manager had a shared responsibility."

In another section of *My Return,* a defense attorney rather euphemistically asks: "Mr. Abbott, did there come a time when you put a knife in the chest of Richard Adan?"

In the book's appendix, Abbott and Zack continue their denial by attempting to make the victim look responsible for his own murder: "Those who knew Adan report that he was aggressive and impatient with strangers. Timidity was not a character trait anyone attributed to Adan, nor has anyone described him as having a sunny disposition. . . . Adan was twenty-two years old, a grown man. . . . He had lived in a violent section of the city for about two years. He knew the streets. He was the same age as the 'Son of Sam' killer. He outweighed Abbott by almost fifty pounds. It was Abbott who knew nothing about Bowery behavior."

This skinny innocent, this naïf, is the same Jack Henry Abbott who wrote in *In the Belly of the Beast:* "Have you ever seen a man despair because he cannot bring himself to murder . . . The only prisoners I have seen who do not despair of being incapable of murder are those who are capable of it." He also wrote: "You have sunk the knife into the middle of his chest. . . . You can feel his life trembling through the knife in your hand. It almost overcomes you, the gentleness of the feeling at the center of a coarse act of murder. You've pumped the knife in several times without even being aware of it. You go to the floor with him to finish him. It is like cutting hot butter. No resistance at all."

In the next chapter, we meet Rochelle, an expert at denial, whose description of the murder committed by the man she loves is one of the most incredible stories in this book.

Rochelle: A Case of Delusion

"He is sensitive to the tiniest of animals"

DEATH ON A SPREE

She had always been a good girl: obedient to her parents, an average student who had earned a bachelor's degree, a loyal friend, a loving fiancée. But when the man she was to marry broke their engagement, she fell apart. She plunged recklessly into a nether world of drinking and drugs, activities that had been only mildly appealing when she was in college. In an attempt to numb her feelings, drugs became her whole life, and there were rumors she used sex to obtain them, that she consorted with the vilest and lowest of characters. One thing is certain: Samantha Lynch was no longer a good girl.

And so she came to spend a night in the winter of 1984 with a young drifter named Duane. They partied at a club and then he invited her back to his place. At thirty, Duane lived occasionally with his mother, at other times with

149

friends; sometimes in jail. He had been convicted of a string of felonies including attempted kidnapping.

Michael E. Knight, currently a judge in California, was the district attorney who would eventually prosecute Duane for murder. He said Duane had been convicted of attempted kidnapping in Las Vegas in 1980: "A woman drove her thirteen- or fourteen-year-old son to school to pick up his books. It was late summer, 1979. While she was sitting in her car in front of the school, [Duane] jumped in, punched her in the face, knocking her against the passenger door, then drove away, saying he would kill her. She was an acrobat or a gymnast and managed to tumble out of the car as he sped away. The next day, after a police pursuit, he crashed the car into a house. He hid under the house but was caught and convicted of attempted kidnapping."

Four years later, Samantha, not knowing and likely not caring about Duane's history, went with him to his mother's apartment. The two snorted cocaine and drank, becoming more and more stoned as the evening went on. When they were about to have sex, Samantha apparently changed her mind, and Duane resorted to force, hitting her with his fists and with a pistol his mother kept in the house. Finally, Samantha's drugged mind told her it was time to sleep; she wanted to go home. She was exhausted and wanted to lay her head down in her own bed. She told Duane she wanted to leave; when they walked out the door, he had his mother's gun in his pocket.

Changing environments was Samantha's fatal mistake. Somewhere between the time she decided she wanted to go home and the next day, she did end up resting, but not in her own bed. By morning's light, Samantha was lying on the hard, cold ground, asleep forever. Duane had killed her.

MURDER ONE

Arrested three days later for Samantha's murder, Duane confessed to police and in a letter to a friend. After a hiatus of three years, Duane was tried for murder, and the then-deputy district attorney of San Fernando, Michael Knight, succeeded in proving Duane guilty.

In California, if the state can prove either that a murder was committed with "malice aforethought" or that it was done during the commission of other felonies, called "special circumstances," a conviction will be first-degree murder for which the sentence can be death. In Duane's case, the prosecutor proved rape and kidnapping—that Duane forced Samantha to drive around with him and that the sex he had with her was, in part, involuntary. Although Knight convinced the jury it was a premeditated, deliberate killing, Duane was spared the death penalty and was given life without parole. The jury was divided on the penalty, with the major dissenting voice belonging to a forty-year-old supermarket cashier who did not believe Duane to be guilty of premeditation or rape and kidnapping. Her name was Rochelle.

THE PROSECUTOR'S TALE

According to Knight, "He tried to have sex with [Samantha] but she locked herself in the bathroom and was trying to climb out the window when he broke the door down. He yanked out the phone wire, then beat and pistol-whipped her. . . . He admits that he had sex with her twice and he admits that he forced her."

The pathologist from the L.A. coroner's office who originally examined Samantha's body said she was pistol-whipped and that there was evidence of sex, but he was not certain she was raped. "I did the autopsy and determined that she had been pistol-whipped and was very concerned that she had been raped. . . . I noticed an abrasion or a roughening of the vaginal lips. . . . There was evidence of sexual activity, but there was no medical proof of rape. . . . There was clear, unequivocal evidence of pistol-whipping. . . . The wound she had to her head had a characteristic pattern—curved lacerations associated with an abrasion on one side [indicating she was] hit with a hard object, usually a gun," said former coroner Terence Allen, M.D.

After they left his mother's apartment, Duane and Samantha got into his truck, but he refused to take her home. "He drove her around with the gun to her head for two or three hours. He took her to a park in a remote area, then shot her in her ear, then in the back of her head. After she was lying on the ground, he shot her in the chest," said Knight.

The prosecutor describes Samantha as religious and studious. "She was engaged to a man who had unceremoniously dumped her. She became lonely and confused." Duane and Samantha likely drank and used cocaine that night. "He gave it to her probably in the hopes she would go to bed with him," said the prosecutor. While he acknowledges that Samantha initially spent time with Duane of her own free will, she ended up trying to get away from him.

In the park, just before dawn, Duane cold-bloodedly "executed" Samantha. As she lay on the ground, he shot her a third time, in the chest. There were contact wounds to Samantha's head, meaning the gun was against her skin when it was fired; the chest wound was made from a distance of a few feet. "I theorize that after she was lying there, still breathing or gurgling or making noises, he then shot her in the chest," said Knight, who believes Duane is a vicious killer. "This man has committed a very callous, cold, terrible criminal act against another human being. . . . He planned the murder and he deliberated over whether or not to do it and he decided to do it. . . . He committed all kinds of acts that showed us he premeditated and thought it out. He formed the intent to kill. He found a place to kill. He executed her. He put the gun in her ear and shot her in the brain."

A SOCIAL TRAGEDY

Duane's defense attorney, Gerald Chaleff, said his client cried when he confessed to police. He said Duane also described the night Samantha died in a letter to a friend. "On the tape, he was crying, was remorseful. . . . He did kill her. He admitted that," said Chaleff.

The legal issue was the degree of murder involved. "I always worried he would be convicted of first-degree murder," said Chaleff. The main problem for the defense attorney and his client was the number of bullets Duane had shot into Samantha's body. In contrast to Michael Knight, Chaleff said the chest wound was made before the head wounds because ballistics reports indicate that it was a clean, round hole with no powder burns. He is also not convinced Samantha was raped. "[Duane] sort of said he had sex with her. She would stop. He said he sort of forced her but she wanted him to."

Also in contrast to the prosecutor, Chaleff does not believe Duane is a killer. "I don't think he is a dangerous human being, an exceptionally violent person. He was under the influence of alcohol and cocaine. If he ever got out, I don't think he'd commit another crime."

Chaleff said the murder was "situational" with "mitigating circumstances." He is completely opposed to Duane's sentence of life without parole, believing it to be a symbol of hopelessness. "I don't think anyone should be sent to prison without parole." What hope is there of rehabilitation if an inmate believes he will never be released no matter how he behaves? But the lawyer acknowledged that Duane murdered a young woman who did not deserve to die. "There should be some punishment. But locking someone up forever is not appropriate. Nothing will ever bring her back."

"AN UNPLANNED SHOOTING THAT
RESULTS IN DEATH"

"He shot a girl but he didn't plan it. It was accidental. . . . When the shooting took place, [Duane] was
drugged out of his mind," said Rochelle, the juror who
stayed the jury's hand, preventing them from sentencing
Duane to death.

Even though she went along with her fellow jurors in
convicting Duane of first-degree murder, she never really
believed him guilty. She caved in, however. "There was too
much pressure. I held out for two weeks, then gave in the
last day. . . . I wished that I'd been a little stronger. . . . I
broke down at the last. . . . All these people believed so
strongly but I didn't see it that way."

Rochelle's tale is radically different from the district
attorney's version of the crime, and somewhat different from
the defense attorney's. She feels quite strongly that Duane
did not receive a fair trial and that he is guilty of, at most,
manslaughter.

"He is responsible for taking a life. *But what happened
is the gun went off when he was not trying to shoot the person,
but trying to fire the gun above the person's head and scare
them."* (Emphasis added.)

"But it had such a heavy trigger pull that by the time
he pulled it down, it was chest level and went off and shot
the girl. . . . A person convicted of an unplanned shooting
that results in death is guilty, not of murder, but of manslaughter.

"I could tell as a juror on his trial that the truth was
not coming out. It was obvious it was so one-sided. . . . He
had been in county jail for three years, and this was his third
set of [appointed] lawyers. . . . The defense attorney was
very weak. . . . He hardly brought anyone in to show the
district attorney's theories were incorrect. . . . [Duane] is
not innocent, but he's not guilty in the way that's charged."

After the trial, Rochelle was so upset by what she felt
was an unfair verdict, she called Duane's attorneys and made

an appointment to visit him in prison. "There was no way I could drop it. . . . After, I came to see just how much was wrong. If [Duane] had had his proper trial, if he had had a decent trial and I felt it was just, I would never have spoken to him. I would never have pursued any of this. I would never have come to know him."

They met. The tall, dark-haired convict and the attractive, redheaded juror. There was instant chemistry. They fell in love, and five months after she helped convict Duane of first-degree murder, Rochelle married him. She was forty-one; he was thirty-four.

THE WIFE'S TALE

Rochelle tells the story of Samantha's death as she heard it from Duane, not as she heard it in the courtroom. She believes the story of Samantha's murder as testified to in court was slanted, tainted, prejudiced against Duane.

Duane and Samantha were together that night, drinking and using cocaine that Samantha procured because she had the connection. Samantha was living in her car off and on and was already a heavy drug user when she met Duane. "She slept around for drugs with various people." After spending some time at Duane's mother's apartment, there was a dispute about sex, and at some point, she hit her head on the showerhead in the bathroom where they were tussling.

Samantha asked to be taken back to her drug dealer's house as she and Duane argued over what was left of the cocaine they had scored earlier. They left the apartment, Duane taking his mother's gun so he could buy ammunition for it. A few days earlier, he had accidentally shot a bullet into the floor under his mother's couch, and that night he remembered to take the gun so he could replace the missing bullet. "He thought, 'I've got to replace the bullet 'cause my mother will see it and get mad.' " Duane and Samantha got into Duane's truck so he could take her home, but she fell asleep. "He wanted to wait until she sobered up some. . . . He wanted to wait until her mind was straight." They drove around for a while, then stopped at a park, got out of the truck, and began walking. Abruptly, Samantha decided to leave Duane and hitch a ride. He told her not to since it was five-thirty in the morning and he offered to take her home. She refused to get into his truck, and in order to convince her, he took out the gun.

"He was going to fire a shot over her head to show her that he meant business. . . . He had a cut on his trigger finger. It had nine stitches on it three days before so it was entirely bandaged up and sticking out straight." He had to use a different finger to pull the trigger. Also, as a juror, Rochelle had felt how heavy the trigger pull was since the gun was part of the trial evidence. "I could hardly pull the trigger back with both hands, it was that heavy a pull. And I imagine if you're drunk and doing drugs, that it would be even more cumbersome." Duane pointed the gun over Samantha's head and tried to pull the trigger, but "by the time he pulled it down, it was chest level and went off and shot the girl. . . . He tells me that part of it is sort of hazy."

In the dim light of near-dawn, the fire that blasted out of the gun was shockingly bright. Duane bent over Samantha. "He heard a gurgling sound and he could hear body fluids leaving her body. He said he knew she was dead but her muscles were trembling. Now this is the part that hung him. Had he gone for help at that moment . . ."

But he didn't, and Rochelle blames his poor judgment on drugs. "A drug specialist said . . . when you're on drugs, especially cocaine . . . you just do the first thing that pops into your mind." In the heat of the moment, Duane recalled an event from his childhood, and according to Rochelle, that memory has cost him his freedom. "When he was a small boy, he remembers his dad backing out of the driveway and running over their puppy. . . . All the kids were upset and everything. . . . His dad said, 'This dog has to be put out of its misery.' . . . He shot it."

Duane performed the same kindness on Samantha. "He

went over to her, knowing that she was dead already but she was still moving. I don't know if he saw blood coming out of her mouth. . . . In his mind, he knew absolutely that she was dying or dead and she was suffering. So he fired two shots to her head. . . . That's a horrible thing, but he thought he was putting her out of her misery. . . . That's not done here in the United States. You don't do that to humans; you do that to animals."

Duane's attorney later said: "If he had only shot her once there wouldn't be an issue. But euthanasia is not a defense."

The police picked up Duane a few days later. Said Rochelle: "He had been drinking and falling down drunk in the park for a week, just waiting for them to pick him up. He knew that sooner or later they'd find him. . . . They picked him up at noon and took a statement from him at one o'clock. He was still drunk. That was the only statement they ever took from him."

Duane hanged himself with his confession. As it is quoted in the *L.A. Times,* he said: "I told her I'd shoot her, and I cocked the gun and when I let go, it went off. . . . I knew I'd hit her, hurt her, so I didn't want her saying anything, I remember thinking at that time, so I just shot her some more."

A ROMANTIC MEETING

After the trial, Rochelle wanted to tell Duane "that someone believed that he wasn't guilty in the manner that he was found guilty. . . . Too many things didn't fit. . . . I wanted to let him know . . . I felt maybe I could say some words to comfort him, to give him the strength to go on and face prison."

She initially visited him in prison to give him some words of comfort and leave some religious tracts with him. She also felt his family and friends were not really supportive during his trial and wanted him to know that someone did care. "I have always been a person who likes to help other people," said Rochelle, who describes herself as God-fearing but not particularly religious. Duane appealed to her desire to be useful and compassionate.

But when she walked into the prison visiting room and saw the man she had watched so closely in the courtroom for the past six months, something more than kindness was kindled. "When I met him face-to-face in the holding prison that day . . . it started to come to me there was far more than I could imagine. . . . I started to see the type of person Duane was. It was overwhelming the injustice [that] was done." Duane told her that he had been shanghaied, railroaded, framed, and his trial had been a distortion of justice. "It was like [my] worst nightmare. Everything I had suspected and could possibly be, was . . . He began to tell me things. . . . He told me he was so discouraged."

Rochelle believes Duane's defense attorney did not represent his best interests. "We were supposed to get to the truth. Not what you think happened, but the truth. . . . Justice was not served. . . . Duane was convicted on what the district attorney said. No one said anything on his behalf; no one brought anything up. [The defense] didn't call in people."

Commiserating on the rotten deal Duane had received, he and Rochelle grew close in that prison visiting room. "I saw a very sensitive and gentle man. When you think of prison, you think of hard-hearted [people] and name-calling, and you think of the toughest, roughest person." But not Duane. "He is sensitive to the tiniest of animals. He's sensitive to nature. He is a very warm, caring, sensitive person that doesn't fit this role at all."

She fell in love, experiencing the deepest feelings she had ever had for a man. Although Rochelle had been married twice, including one seventeen-year relationship that gave her two children, she believes she had never loved before. "Very few people ever really love. There are lots of people you can meet and be compatible with. This has happened to me in my life many times before." But Duane struck her like a bolt of lightning. "It's entirely different. All the other possessions, all the other things in life, mean very little. What I want is to be with him." They married in late 1988.

"To say that I love him is not enough. Love doesn't cover it . . . doesn't even scratch the surface. . . . I adore him. I love and adore him."

"This is stranger than fiction," said Deputy District Attorney Knight in the *L.A. Times.* "She apparently fell in love with the guy during the trial. I've seen some jurors become enamored of the guy, but I've never seen where they've actually gone and met the guy and married him."

For the first time, Rochelle is passionately in love. But she will neither lie in his arms nor live in a house with him; she will not cook dinner or raise children or do any of the many large and small acts that make up a marriage. Rochelle will live alone and Duane will spend his years inside the walls of a state penitentiary. Although they share the deepest love, they will not be permitted to be together except for two six-hour visits a week.

The dead body of Samantha Lynch lies between them. And always will.

AT HOME IN TENNESSEE

Mom was from a tiny village in Tennessee and Dad was a big-city barkeep. For a few years they lived over Rochelle's father's bar in Detroit, but eventually Mom put her foot down, and the family, minus Dad, moved back to Tennessee.

Dad lived above the bar because it was convenient for a man with a sixteen-hour workday; it was the only life he had ever known. He had no interest in moving to a rural town with a population of 250 and living off the land. But Mom hated the big city. It was just about the worst place in the world to raise children, she thought. Rochelle was conceived one summer when her mother and brother visited Detroit, but her pregnant mother returned to Tennessee anyway.

Mom and Dad visited back and forth when Rochelle was very young. "He was always in and out of my life until I was three. Then my mother decided, 'No. No more.' " Dad was "business minded," refusing to give up his bar and move to the country, so Mom built her own house on land her parents gave her, using money her absent husband sent. When the house was finished, she moved in and never left. Life was simple, almost spartan. Mom made the children's clothing and fed them from her garden. When Rochelle's brother got older, he hunted and supplied the family with meat.

Mom and Dad never divorced. Rochelle spent summers in Detroit until she was nine, then the visits stopped, but Dad wrote every week. Rochelle did not feel his absence much. Mom was everything. Rochelle adopted all of her mother's ideas, values, fears, and hopes. "I never felt I was missing out particularly. I never had any fantasies. My father just wasn't there. We didn't even want to go to visit him in Detroit because the country life was better than the city life. [In Detroit] we couldn't go out on the sidewalks because my mother worried that someone would snatch us."

Gradually Rochelle and her father drifted apart; he became a fading memory of "a nice man." She would have enjoyed more visits, but not on his turf. Like Mom, she despised the city. "I would have liked to have had him in the country, but not in that environment. . . . There was always lots of trash on the sidewalk and dirt and spit." Dad, so reluctant to leave Detroit and move to Tennessee, relocated to Florida "to get out of the cold" when Rochelle was a teenager. She visited him once in Florida. She was fourteen and only noticed, with surprise, that he was short.

Rochelle's self-sufficient mother is her role model, the person she most admires. "My mother has very strong beliefs. She's religious but not a fanatic. . . . She just has a basic good sense about the way life is. She's a simple person, not cluttered or complicated by worldly possessions. . . . She doesn't need a new car to make her happy. She believes in God, in raising her family, in doing the right thing by others . . . in doing right, not doing wrong. . . . She's a laughing and loving person, but very strict."

Mom still lives alone in her house in the middle of forty acres but is so strong spiritually and emotionally that "she doesn't need to have people around her to feel of value. . . . She doesn't need other people to satisfy her. She's satisfied with herself."

Mom has one fault, though, a shortcoming one would expect in a self-sufficient, strong countrywoman: She minces no words. "She's cut-to-the-bone outspoken. She doesn't cover anything over. She just says the way she feels." While Mom's single flaw fits her personality, that did not help Rochelle while she was growing up. She was often embarrassed in front of her friends by her mother's sharp tongue.

Despite this one problem, Rochelle recalls her childhood as extremely full and happy. "I never really felt the need for a father 'cause my mother was everything. She was a strong, together person. Other than the fact of a father's presence in the house, I never knew, I never thought, that a father could make any difference because my mother did everything." Childhood was picture perfect: "the American home, out on the farm, good country living, the family sitting down to the dinner table at night all together . . ."

FIRST MARRIAGE

Although her life was "perfect," at the tender age of seventeen with her senior year of high school still unfinished, Rochelle decided to leave home and see the world, believing the only way to do that was to marry. With Mom's blessings, she married a man six years older. He took Rochelle away from the small village of her idyllic childhood, but the marriage was such a disaster that six weeks later it was annulled and she returned home to finish high school.

After graduation, she made a more successful attempt to leave home, making it all the way to California, traveling with relatives and living with them until she got settled. She began working in a restaurant and soon started dating Pierre, a coworker who was seventeen years older. When they married after three years, Rochelle was twenty-one and Pierre was thirty-eight.

As her second husband, Pierre was the father she never had and the teacher she desperately needed. Being more sophisticated, he had knowledge and experience that his wife soaked up eagerly. They had two children together. They had a tranquil life, never arguing, working together to get ahead.

When Rochelle was in her thirties, she began to feel that she wanted more than Pierre could offer, more passion, more excitement. "We never fought. It wasn't a bad situation, but I knew there should be more to life. I had really outgrown him. . . . I just wanted to branch out, to explore the world." They stayed together for several years more, sleeping in separate bedrooms and finally separating when Rochelle was thirty-eight and Pierre fifty-five.

When they separated, Rochelle found no shortage of interested men. She dated a lot and had three serious relationships. Finally, she decided to marry again even though her fiancé, like all the other men she knew, just never seemed totally right. "Men have cared more for me than I cared for them. I always ended up seeing something in them that I didn't care for. I just never really found the person that I really wanted."

She compromised as she had with Pierre and was living with her fiancé while she was a juror in Duane's trial. Her fiancé didn't believe in God, though, and that was a real problem because in order for her to truly love a man, he must "have a relationship with God."

TRUE LOVE

"When I met Duane, nothing that had ever been before could even compete with my feelings." To Rochelle, Duane is worthy of her adoration because he is more than a regular man. Men have always been imperfect to Rochelle. She could never quite find the right one, the one who would arouse in her the passionate enchantment of deep, romantic love. But she can love Duane because he is the perfect victim who inspires in her noble and pure feelings. She will be his crusader: saving him, fighting the system, making any sacrifice necessary.

Duane was raised by a neglectful, alcoholic family. Later, he was victimized by the imperfect and heartless California criminal justice system. He was even a victim of the woman he murdered: She supplied the cocaine; she sold her body for drugs; and finally, she refused to get in his truck, forcing him to shoot her.

Duane has convinced Rochelle that he is kind, gentle, sensitive, and believes in God. He told her that his morality and ethics are the same as hers; they are two sides of the same coin. "He is the male version of me. He is myself, but he is a man. . . . We have the same feelings. It's amazing how much alike we are and how sensitive we are in the same areas. . . . We feel the same about . . . moral issues, life around us, love and family." But there is something confusing here: Even if Duane did not intend to murder Samantha, his actions still don't fit in with Rochelle's proclaimed values. What is she doing with a man who used a gun in order to "scare" someone? With a man who's used drugs?

ROCHELLE'S DENIAL

Despite what she heard and saw as a juror, Rochelle has chosen to ignore evidence and testimony so she can believe what Duane told her. Her denial is necessary for maintenance of her fantasy; she has to believe his version of what happened so she can continue to love him.

By saving Duane, Rochelle can shore up the rough edges of her own psyche. By battling the California justice system, Rochelle is David fighting Goliath, truth and right battling injustice. If she can win—or even if she can maintain the fight—she will prove that she is "right" and "good," that her mother was the perfect mother, that she had the perfect childhood. She can prove that life really is wonderful. That bad things don't happen to good people. That people don't kill for no good reason. That life is not arbitrary and capricious. That life is orderly, good, clean, healthy, and all the other Girl Scout adjectives by which Rochelle has precariously lived for forty-three years.

She has tentatively balanced her idealized childhood, her fantasy of her mother, her illusions about the world, her idealistic view of life—with what she saw and heard in a California courtroom. She won't acknowledge ugliness because it threatens her fragile defense mechanism. She won't admit what she saw and heard in the courtroom: That people do drugs. They have sex. They beat each other. They rape, kill, and lie.

If Rochelle can crusade for Duane so forcefully and convincingly that she saves him from the steely jaws of prison, she can validate herself.

SACRIFICE

"I gave up almost everything." First, her fiancé. Then, her daughter and son, sending them to live with her ex-husband, then with her mother in Tennessee. "My son wouldn't speak to me; he was nine. My daughter had just graduated from high school. It was a hard time for her even without this. She went to stay with my mother." Crusaders set out on missions knowing they will inevitably make major sacrifices. Rochelle is no different.

"I knew this was what I wanted, and I knew I had to cut a lot of ties . . . and I did. . . . I wanted to give him myself," said Rochelle on a segment of the syndicated television show "The Reporters." On the same show, her children related the effect on them of their mother's relationship with Duane. Her daughter said, "I cried . . . I got emotional . . . I thought she was giving everything up. . . . I didn't think she was treating my brother and I the right way." Rochelle's son said the whole experience "was really awful."

Eventually, Rochelle gave up her home, moving to be near Duane's prison. She has also sacrificed countless hours of her time, waiting on line to get into the prison for visits. The first year Duane was in prison, Rochelle visited 300 out of 360 days. Why the sacrifice? an interviewer on "The Reporters" asked. "Because he enjoys it. Because he's so appreciative of every effort I make."

She gave up her privacy, allowing her story to be told on television. She almost lost Mom, who initially disapproved of Duane. "I was bitterly opposed. I thought he might get out and even kill her," said her mother on "The Reporters."

Rochelle is "very delusional. She went into the trial deluded—that much badness just couldn't exist. For her to recognize the truth would destroy her concept of the world. . . . She has to recreate [Duane] as a good person, so she has to put the blame on the system," said psychiatrist Dr. Neil Kaye.

Because she never rebelled against her mother, a natural part of the maturation process, she is unable to "grow up as a woman and differentiate herself from her mother," added the psychiatrist. So she fantasizes about returning to Tennessee, with Duane, to live on the land as her mother does. She wants to go back to the womb, the mother earth. Rochelle has to confirm the picture her mother painted of the world. If she finds out the world is grays—not black-and-white—her belief system will crack.

FANTASY: AFTER PRISON

Rochelle and Duane are sitting on the front porch of their house. It's made of wood planks that Duane cut from trees growing on their own land. They eat fresh vegetables from their garden and fruit from their own trees. The house is furnished simply with furniture Duane built and curtains and cushions made by Rochelle.

"Should he get out, we would go back and live on a piece of ground and work in the garden and live a simple life. . . . We would do the simplest of things, go to church, be close to our families. . . . He is a welder and a carpenter. If we didn't live in the city and didn't pay rent, we wouldn't need that much money. . . . There's trees and lumber and we could always build a house."

Her fantasy of a pioneer/farmer existence for the two of them is delusional considering Duane has a prison record that began when he was in his teens; his crimes progressed from burglaries to use of a weapon to murder. His probation officer wrote: "He seems unwilling or unable to do anything to alter his pattern of criminality. . . . Cannot live in a civilized society. . . . Criminality seems to increase . . . remorseless . . . also intelligent and articulate." Also, it's unlikely Duane will be freed since he's serving life without parole.

In Rochelle's mind, Duane's good values were distorted by his family's bad influence, so she's trying to remake his terrible past. "I've tried to be an example of goodness and cleanliness to his family. I don't want to be a saint or anything, but they've done all the wrong things."

SAINT ROCHELLE

Truth is, she does want to be a saint, and according to one prison official, she acts like one. "I don't think this guy knows what he has—a treasure. She truly believes that with her love and support, he can change. [Rochelle] is an archangel," said Lt. Cammy Voss, public information officer at Folsom Prison. "We think there are fifty states, but women have more than fifty. We have fifty-one . . . a State of Hope." Rochelle is living in that fifty-first state, believing that her love will change Duane and will even clean the slate of his past transgressions. "He has not been a good boy, but he is not a criminal, not a killer," said Rochelle.

By making Duane her cause, Saint Rochelle takes two empty, unfulfilled lives—his and hers—and gives them purpose and meaning. "The guy is almost irrelevant at this point. He's a dream lover, a phantom limb," said clinical psychologist Stuart Fischoff, Ph.D. Although her relationship with Duane is the most exquisite love affair of her life, she'll never share real intimacy with him. And that's okay because up until now, as she has said, men have disappointed her—just as her father did. There's been something "wrong" with all of her previous relationships. But Duane can't disappoint her. He's whoever she wants him to be. Saint Rochelle and her fantasy prince will live happily ever after.

Little Girl Lost

*"Once I said, 'Daddy, don't yell.' He
hit me with the buckle end of the
belt"*

Like Rochelle, women who love killers are only *acting*
the role of women in love. The men they love are not real;
they are fantasies created by the women's psychological and
emotional needs. But on the surface, there are similarities
between these women and "women who love too much" in
their behavior in relationships and in their family histories.
Like "women who love too much," women who fall for
murderers generally came from dysfunctional families. Each
woman was, as a child, a little girl lost. "Their internal script
for how you have a relationship is one of pathology," said
Dr. Janet Warren, a forensic social worker who studies murderers and their relationships.

The majority of the women interviewed for this book
were abused during their childhoods, physically, emotionally, and/or sexually. They lived in families where little love
was shared. The suffering these women endured as children
eradicated parts of their psyches. For some, their souls were
killed—"soul murder," according to psychiatrist Leonard

Shengold, M.D., author of *Soul Murder: The Effects of Childhood Abuse and Deprivation.*

"The horror and violence of murder are immediately apparent. But not all violence, not all murder, indeed, is physical. Violence done to the emotions can destroy us as thoroughly as a blow; faith, love and trust can be murdered as well as people," wrote Alison Hennegan in her introduction to *Reader, I Murdered Him: Original Crime Stories by Women.*

Children, so sensitive to hurt, can easily be destroyed. "The effect on them of torture, hatred, seduction, and rape—or even of indifference and withholding love and care—is usually the devastating one of developmental arrest, for their souls, their psychological structure and functioning, are still forming," writes Shengold.

Chronic, repeated abuse has the effect of suppressing the mechanism that allows us to feel happy, to trust, to love, and to care about others. This is why so many abused girls grow up to be women who can't really love but must form illusory relationships with inappropriate men—such as murderers. These women often went directly from abusive childhood homes to marriage, at very young ages, to men who were abusive physically, emotionally, and/or sexually.

Women who love killers generally had terrible relationships with all men, in addition to the poor relationships with their husbands and fathers. They were raped, sexually assaulted, and attacked by men; they were used by men and often saw themselves as victims.

Many of these women experienced loss during their childhoods: the death of either a parent or a close relative. Loving a murderer allows a woman to experience endless repetition of loss; her beloved will never be with her and she feels this loss on a daily basis. This is acceptable because it is familiar.

Every woman interviewed for this book described, in varying degrees, some pathology in her childhood. These ranged from the woman who was raped at age five by her father, to the woman who was daddy's girl until she needed his protection from the husband who was so abusive he broke her bones, to the woman whose "perfect childhood" was spent with a mother who was mentally ill, to the woman whose mother committed suicide.

The most commonly seen structure of the childhood families of these women—a domineering, often alcoholic father and a submissive mother—lends itself to abuse and dysfunction. After a while, it seemed to me as if everyone I interviewed had been abused; every woman had a "horror" story to tell. "As soon as you start working with criminals and their women, you begin to think everyone has been abused," said forensic psychiatrist Park Dietz.

With a few exceptions, the women interviewed for this book were raised in families where the father was dominant. For other women, raised without fathers, mothers took on the role of authoritarian and ruled the roost as firmly, and repressively, as any man. But for the most part, the father was the focus of the family.

FATHER

He was the boss; his opinions were not questioned either by his wife or his children. He worked and brought his paycheck home to support his family while his wife stayed at home and ran the house. The family was centered around his desires, needs, and availability. Dinner was eaten when he arrived home from work, no matter the hour. If he was in a bad mood, mother was quieter than usual and the children had to keep out of sight. If father was feeling okay, good times were in order.

"The entire family revolved around him, our little nuclear family, my mother and the girls. . . . I remember the last time that he beat me. I remember feeling that I had a power, that if I didn't cry out . . . I didn't, and that upset him terribly. He told my mother, 'I can't reach her anymore.'

I felt cold rage. . . . I stood there like a piece of stone. That was the last time he ever beat me." (Francine, married to Charlie)

In the families of most of the women interviewed, fathers were more than family heads. They were domineering, controlling little czars, brooking no autonomy or independence in anyone else, including their wives. They were frequently cruel; they beat their daughters. Some had sex with them.

"I was sexually abused by my father [when I was] five years old. . . . My mother knew. . . . She hated me and I hated her. . . . She wouldn't let me sleep at night. She would throw water on me. I'd have to get up, change my pajamas, change everything. Then she'd throw water on me again. . . . She would take a top off a pot and put it over my head and bang it. She would make me lie on the hard floor. . . . Now when I look back at it, now that I understand it, I see that's why she hated me. He was her man." (Lori, in love with Kevin)

Many fathers of the women interviewed were alcoholics. Francine was beaten on a regular basis throughout her childhood by her alcoholic father, who was also harshly critical of her and psychologically cruel. As a child, Francine fantasized that eventually her father would stop drinking and stop beating her, and that her passive, withdrawn mother would become a loving, nurturing parent. This is wrong, she thought. It all should be perfect, the way it is on TV. Now, as an adult, Francine is trying to "make it perfect" by living an illusion, by having a "love" relationship with a "perfect" man, a man of her own creation.

Children raised in families where abuse is the norm often end up retreating into fantasy because reality is too painful. The child has nowhere to go, no place to hide, so she opts out of real life. "How much more oppressed can you be than to not be able to walk on the earth as your own person? It's literally that, psychologically, she has never gotten the chance to be born," said psychotherapist Charlotte Kasl, Ph.D., author of *Women, Sex and Addiction.*

"I can remember going for a week without really eating," said Lori. There was no help; she thought about calling the police but never did. "I was so afraid of my father, of what he would do. He could kill me. He probably would have."

If a woman can come out of a tortured childhood without cracking up, without going off the deep end, it means she has successfully developed sophisticated defense mechanisms. Falling in love with a killer is one of those defenses; it's a way of having a relationship without ever having to get too close. Women who fall in love with murderers are trying to do over their troubled childhoods. They say to themselves: "I will make it perfect. I will fall in love with a man who can't drink and can't beat me. He'll always be there for me because he really needs me." The love affair takes place behind prison walls and the man she loves has committed murder, *but he's under her control.* Her compulsive need to be loved by a man she can control, who can't hurt her, leads her to love a man who will never get out of prison, who will never have any real power in their relationship. No, daddy won't ever get a chance to hurt her again.

MISSING FATHERS

Instead of abusive fathers, women who love convicted killers may have had missing or absent fathers—unavailable to them for a variety of reasons. Some were workaholics. Others died. Often a divorce would mean the father dropped out of sight and the child lost her relationship with him.

Dolores, whose boyfriend, Louis, is serving life without parole for murder, was her father's pet. "He spoiled me quite a bit. . . . I was always his little girl. I was the only one that he let drive his cars, that he let help in the store. . . . Even today, he relies on me more than he does the other ones. . . . I used to go out of my way a lot for him. I would bake cakes for him and make special things for him. . . . I always wanted him to be proud of me."

He was basically an absent father. A workaholic who put in fifteen to eighteen hours every day, he was home only for dinner, then he went back to his business. Dolores achieved excellent grades to please her father. "It seemed that he was so busy all the time working that I had to get good grades in school and be on the honor roll. . . . When he was home, it was nice to be able to have good things to show him, to talk about." Dolores became an object to her father and to herself; she lost touch with her self, lost self-esteem, lost ego, unless she was performing and achieving to please Father.

Despite the fact that her mother—with whom Dolores got along well—ran the family since her father was never there, he was still the head of the house. "He was the boss. . . . Anything major, he would handle. . . . He would look at you in a certain way and you would know what was happening." Dolores's mother, true to her Catholicism, didn't inform Dolores about sex as a physical act. "I knew only how babies were made and how you got your period."

Despite her academic achievement, Dolores skipped college and married at eighteen. Her choice was unfortunate: an alcoholic and a womanizer, eight years older than Dolores. She was a virgin, ignorant about sex. He raped her repeatedly for the first few years of their marriage. The marriage fell apart when her husband began beating their son. "When he was drunk, he was very mean. . . . When [our son] was three or four years old, he would beat him up, abuse him very badly." He threatened Dolores, also. Finally, he told her he had developed an obsession for young girls and that he had molested several girls—including Dolores's niece.

What does daddy's girl do when she's in trouble? It

didn't work in this case. "My father's attitude was, 'You make your bed, you sleep in it.' He actually said that when I got married. Mother didn't have very much to say about it. She was very much under my father's thumb." Dolores divorced her husband when their son was eleven, then moved out of state. Neither her father nor her mother had ever come to her aid.

A PERFECT CHILDHOOD

Like many people whose families were dysfunctional, women who love killers often hide the truth about their childhoods because their pain is too enormous to confront. These women, masters at denial, learn at mother's knee how to deny that which is painful. When Hilary's husband beat her brutally, her parents refused to acknowledge what was happening. She pretended she'd walked into a door and they pretended to believe her.

Women who love murderers use their childhood ability to deny in their adult relationships. Even for the women who claim to have had happy childhoods, something seems amiss. Annette, married to a career criminal convicted of murder, said she had "a happy childhood. . . . I'm so fortunate." But something went wrong in her development. The oldest of four children, she was brought up in a "close-knit" Catholic family that emphasized "careers, getting a job, doing a good job." The children's education, apparently, left out sex. At age forty-eight, Annette is still a virgin and she's very proud of it. The boys, and later the men, she dated during her life were interested in sex; she never was.

What mattered to her were work and career. And when she finally fell in love, at age thirty-eight, it was with Jack, who was serving two consecutive prison sentences: first, twenty-five to forty years for wounding a police officer; and second, a life sentence for murder. Annette's virginity is safe: Jack won't be making sexual advances during this lifetime.

MOTHERS

Even if fathers wielded most of the power, mothers, too, could be highly destructive presences. One woman who claims a "perfect childhood," Carla, is maried to a Florida death-row inmate. After Carla's parents divorced when she was three, she visited her father but spent most of her time with her mother. When her father remarried a short time later, Carla didn't like her stepmother "because my mother was resentful" and tried to make Carla dislike the new woman in her father's life. Today, Carla says her stepmother is a "nice, good person, but I didn't like her then."

Although Carla identified closely with her mother, she was also angry at her and blamed her for the divorce. "My father was a good man and she kicked him out; she didn't want to be married."

Carla's mother "had a history of mental problems. She wasn't that rational. She just had her lapses. I didn't know it, but before I was born, she was in a mental hospital." While Carla was growing up, her mother had no breakdowns that Carla remembers, except she continually tried to influence Carla to stop loving her father. "She would always say he was a terrible man; she tried to turn us against him."

When this little girl lost grew up, social drinking rapidly "got out of control." She described herself as "a little depressed and an alcoholic" when she met her murderer/husband, Martin. Now, she's helped him and he's helped her. "I don't drink or smoke anymore," said Carla.

Sometimes, mothers act in a domineering and repressive manner, inspiring love-hate feelings in their bewildered and overpowered daughters. Rochelle had such a mother. Another domineering mother is described by Elena, whose husband was executed a few years ago.

Her mother was an attorney, "intelligent, domineering, very repressive, very controlling. I wasn't even allowed to go to Sunday school class. She was definitely the head of the household." Father, twenty-three years older than Mother, "thought she was a gift from heaven. . . . Anything she did was all right." She didn't bother to hide her affairs—everyone knew the names of her lovers and Father even baby-sat when she went out. Mother always told Elena she wasn't good enough. When the child was thirteen, she had enough, went to live with her grandmother, and married a year later when she was fourteen.

Domineering mothers are a minority, however, in the families of women who love killers. Generally, the typical dysfunctional family described by these women consists of a bossy, often abusive father and a passive mother who knuckles under to his demands. Mother passes on to her daughters a legacy of low self-esteem, self-doubt, and nonassertive behavior. She can't protect her daughter from being beaten because she can't protect herself. Her behavior, and that of her husband, reinforces sex-role stereotypes to her young daughter. She is woman as victim, and her daughter models from her. These mothers are themselves so intimidated, they can't protect their daughters from rape, incest, physical batterings, emotional abuse. Sometimes they share in the abuse because, by participating, they create the fantasy that they have some control over their own lives.

The ultimate threat of a domineering, cruel father and a passive mother is that the father will eventually turn to his daughters for sexual gratification.

Says Francine, "My father was very invasive in his questioning of my feelings and development and in telling me the kinds of things that were going to happen to me. He deliberately went around the house with no clothes on. It upset me and my sisters, [but] he said that sexuality was a natural healing experience and he didn't want his girls excited because they never saw a man before. . . . If you were going to be punished, he was likely to call you in for the lecture as he took a shower and then got out and shaved—all of which he did without his clothes on."

EMOTIONAL ABUSE

Emotional abuse is a catchall term to describe all the wrong things parents do to children. It's normal for a parent to lose control once in a while, but a child brought up in a household where parents are constantly berating the child—faulting, criticizing, blaming, putting down, insulting—will suffer great damage. Many women who love convicted killers described damaging relationships with parents, from outright cruelty to the opposite extreme—overpossessive, suffocating "love."

REPETITION

The great majority of women interviewed for this book were married by seventeen or eighteen, even those who said they had "happy" or "perfect" childhoods. Many of the women married men who displayed the very qualities they so despised in their fathers. This repetition is to be expected when a parent is so authoritarian that the child can't develop her own will; she takes on the will of her parent. The child, later a woman, with no will or self of her own, internalizes the beliefs of the parent or parents who abused her.

A majority of women who love men who kill have had severely abusive relationships with men *before* they met their murderer/lovers. Each killer is therefore a safe haven because he is locked up, a respite to the woman who has been so brutalized previously. He is also a repetition of the abusive father because he has, after all, murdered.

Says Dolores, "My first husband was emotionally abusive and threatened me with death. He beat the kids. The second marriage, we argued all the time; it was a turbulent relationship."

Kay's live-in boyfriend would become "very violent. He threatened my life." When she tried to move out of their apartment, he threatened her until she became afraid he would kill her. "We had an oil lamp. He said, 'I want to tie you up and just let this lamp turn over and burn you to death.' " Kay did not want to have sex with him because of his abusive behavior, so he would rape her—"but not really because I would give in."

When she finally left him, he pulled the cruelest trick of all—emotional blackmail, showing friends pictures of the two of them engaging in oral sex from an earlier, happier time. He even threatened to show the pictures to her son. "I had to get my phone number changed, but he found out where I lived. . . . I got an [order of protection] out on him and that helped some. Then his mother, his own mother, begged me to take him back."

What a relief it was for Kay to meet Ruben! A convicted murderer, doing life, he was handsome and exciting—and behind bars.

Elena had four children with a man who ran around with other women and neglected his family. "He didn't want the responsibility. He also discovered he was attractive to other women and began philandering." That first marriage soured Elena toward men. Between the time she divorced at age twenty-five and the fateful day thirteen years later when she fell in love with death-row inmate Terry, she had no serious long-term relationships.

LOW SELF-ESTEEM

The more awful the childhood, the less self, or identity, develops in each individual because a child's identity and self-esteem depend, in large part, on her feeling that she is cared about, that she has a nurturing, all-knowing parent who can right wrongs. How can a woman think anything of herself if her parents didn't? How can she love herself if she was criticized, abused, and belittled? How can she have a positive self-image if she was a member of a family whose female role model, mother, was a weak, impotent creature who did father's bidding?

Women who love killers take low self-esteem to its furthest reaches: I wasn't worth anything to my parents. I'm not worth anything to me. So I'll go after someone that society has branded unacceptable. "I would be amazed if they weren't among the neediest and most dependent of women. As in the transference cure in psychoanalysis, the women are sucking up a part of the men's egos and that gives them the illusion of being in control. . . . So by identifying with the popular stereotype of the tough guy, they feel stronger," said psychiatrist Park Dietz.

In truth, though, murderers are weak, not strong. "Murderers are losers," added Dietz. The strength of a murderer is an illusion; the idea that he is tough is a fantasy. But these women are so used to living lies, they don't see the weaknesses in the men they love. As children, they were players in a big charade presented by their families, an illusion they had to maintain in public, in school, with their friends. Don't tell anyone that daddy beats you. Don't tell anyone that mommy pours water on your head in the middle of the night. Pretend that everything is fine. Pretend mommy and daddy love you, that you're secure, that you are safe in their care. Women who love convicted killers are pros at maintaining illusions.

"These women live in a different reality with a different emotional system. . . . Any of the elements—an alcoholic father, an abusive father—could warp her view of men so she would pursue a totally nonrational attraction to men," said psychologist Stuart Fischoff. Each woman will use her love as a way to (falsely) boost her self-esteem. "She tells herself, 'I'm offering myself to a man who is in jail so I will become an extremely special person.' "

One woman, quoted in *Ebony* magazine, explained how special her murderer/lover made her feel. "I wasn't looking for a husband, but there was something about him that attracted me, and I liked it," said Zettye Price, who married convicted murderer Willie Bates in 1980. They met four years earlier when she and her minister went into a state penitentiary in Mississippi to talk to the inmates. "I think everyone needs someone, and he's the person I needed because he loves and appreciates me." Willie Bates may have been a murderer, but he made Zettye Price feel loved and cared about. For women with low self-esteem, that is the most important aspect of any love relationship.

Victims, Repeaters, Rebels

"I went to a bar once, when I was eighteen, and came out when I was twenty-eight"

VICTIMS

Many women who love murderers learned victim behavior during their childhoods and were launched early in victim careers. "Loving an inmate who's in [prison] for life is . . . victimization because these marriages cannot deliver a stable intimate relationship with another mature adult," said Dr. Dietz.

Women who love convicted killers are partly attracted to these men because, subconsciously, they want to remain victims. The women are aware, on some deep level, that they are being used. They are not getting all they could out of a love relationship. They will never enjoy sex, companionship, the joys of a loving marriage. But these women are so convinced they should remain victims because they don't deserve anything better that they maintain the fiction that they are happy. As children, they learned to live lies; now,

181

as women, they continue lying and pretending—to themselves, as well as to everyone else.

Says Francine, "As I look back on it, I see that was my perception of myself, that first I had been powerless with respect to my father, then I was powerless with respect to my husband. Finally I realized—you are going to have to quit clutching all these hurts to your bosom. . . . Pain is like a shield and it protects you from the outside world. . . . But the only way you can ever get out of this place is to give up the luxury of the pain that you've suffered."

As a child victim, being beaten was preferable to being forgotten. Women who were abused as children develop a victim mentality, often causing them to confuse beatings with feelings of endearment. The beatings can even be gratifying because they can be viewed, in a twisted way, as proof of affection: Better battered than ignored.

Women who love murderers also mix up endearment, love, affection, and attention with violence. Dancing with a master of death has its allure. Not only the potent attractiveness of a violence that is confused with strength, but the violence that each woman remembers from her childhood, violence connected with attention and love.

REPEATERS

Children who are abused must deal with the often remorseful, apologetic parents who hurt them. A child will have mixed feelings after an abusive episode if her parent expresses regrets: She will feel angry and hurt, but she will also feel guilt and love. Over and over, this is repeated, sometimes on a daily basis. Eventually the child begins to feel there is some connection between love and pain. She learns that if she feels hurt first, love and hugs will come later.

As an adult, she may seek a relationship that repeats this pattern of pain/hurt first, followed by love/affection. She may grow to love a man who abuses her because it's the only kind of love she has known. Repeatedly, women who love killers told me about abusive parents, boyfriends, and husbands. Now, in their relationships with murderers, although they are safe from abuse because the murderers are behind bars, there is still a basic underlying threat, a potent danger lurking just below the surface. These men have killed and could kill again. They represent the greatest potential threat of abuse. The women are repeating the love-pain connection they learned as children in their relationships with murderers.

Many women who love men who kill suffer from repetition compulsion and "are trying to rework their pasts to finally conquer the unapproachable fathers," said Dr. Fischoff.

Francine's case is one of the most bizarre. Of all the women interviewed, she was one of the worst victims of physical abuse. Yet the father who brutalized her and her murderer/husband share the same first name, so she is constantly reminded of her father. "She is struggling desperately to replace her father," said psychiatrist Neil Kaye. "If [Charlie] is her father, she finally has the chance to turn the tables. She finally can control him the way her father controlled her." When Francine's father died, she felt sorry for him because he had been very sick. That pity is not unlike the feeling she has for Charlie, according to Dr. Kaye: "He has a little problem called killing, and her father had a little problem called drinking."

REBELS

Some women who love murderers are rebels, creating drama out of the stuff of their everyday lives because they have no other outlet for feelings of aggression and daring. Because their self-image is so weak, they are attracted by a life on the edge. These women reject what is culturally endorsed and are attracted to what's deviant. *Sheer badness* attracts them; they are "good girls" attracted to "bad boys."

For the rebel, excitement and drama make life worthwhile, and chaos substitutes for warmth and affection. In
The Agony of It All, Joy Davidson writes: "In the titillation
of rebellion, we are buttressed by the irrational belief that
we are special, that we can get away with it." The sheer
outrageousness of loving a man who has murdered causes a
woman to transcend her feelings of low self-esteem, of vulnerability. The thrill of her relationship makes her feel alive
and important. By controlling the melodramatic events in
their lives, women who love men who kill get a false and
temporary sense of power.

Alicia, in love with Bill, who murdered another man
during a knife fight, began rebelling in college by using rec-
reational drugs. "One of the reasons college was so intense
for me was that my background was so dull. [College] was
like winding up in Disneyland." Whatever she was running
from, it kept her going for twenty-five years. During college,
she had no focus and was interested mainly in playing. She
had fun and worked at easy jobs just to pay the bills. "I went
to a bar once, when I was eighteen, and came out when I
was twenty-eight." Finally, "I just got sick of being drunk,
of having hangovers. All my friends were partying. . . . My
life was at a dead end. I wasn't going anywhere."

In the years since, Alicia tried to find a center by taking
college courses and working, but she never found what she
was seeking. She was a drifter of sorts, living in six different
states, working in a dozen fields. When she met and fell in
love with Bill, she became focused, chose a career, went
back to school, and is now working full-time plus twenty
hours a week to support the two of them.

Alicia is not aware that choosing Bill as a lovemate is
a continuation of her lost, lonely drifting and that she is still
a rebel. If anything, she has found an even better way to
live on the edge; dancing with a master of death provides
about as much risk as anyone could handle. As it does with
other rebels, the drama in Alicia's love relationship takes
the place of real intimacy and closeness. By loving Bill, she

is able to experience dramatic conflict, challenge, and excitement.

He is her biker, her Hell's Angel, her Mick Jagger—the bad boy she was warned against. For middle-class women especially, loving a murderer can be very attractive because it satisfies inner needs for intensity, excitement, and risk taking.

Lori: A Case of Desperation

"He called me his princess"

LORI

One night when Lori was five, her father climbed into her bed. He sexually abused her repeatedly until she was eight. By then, Lori's spirit had died; she was a victim of "soul murder." Her spirit was killed by incest, beatings, and emotional abuse on the part of her father. And her mother! Her mother sometimes woke Lori in the middle of the night by pouring water on her. Both parents were alcoholics and both abused their daughter.

When Lori was thirty-eight, she considered killing herself. Her life had been an agony of loneliness, suffering, and pain, a long march toward nowhere. She had never had anyone to love; no one had given her any love. Her husband of twenty years didn't respond to her with affection. She had no children. Waitressing for a living gave her no real satisfaction. What was there to live for?

Lori's husband said he was "not interested in her as a

woman." He humiliated and belittled her. He didn't allow
her to write checks; other than her income as a waitress, she
had no access to any money. She cooked, cleaned, and ad-
ministered her husband's daily asthma medication. The few
friends she made in the fundamentalist church she belonged
to advised her to stay with her husband even though she
wasn't happy. Where else can you go? they asked. And
because she had little education and few job skills, Lori
stayed. Besides, since her spirit had been killed as a child,
she was not one to make changes.

Lori plodded on, sadly, hopelessly. But she never broke
down. One day, on television, she heard someone talking
about taking life "one day at a time," and that's how she
made it through the endless days and nights. "I'd get up in
the morning and I would say, 'Well, I'll go to lunch without
thinking about my father, thinking about other things.' And
I did it. Then I would go from lunch to dinner. . . . And I
kept doing that, day in, day out, day in, day out. And it did
ease the pain. I can remember someone saying to me, 'Time
heals all wounds.' I thought, 'Are you kidding?' But it's true.
The weeks turn to months, the months to years. The pain
isn't the same."

Lori sat down one morning during her break and began
to thumb through a copy of *The Village Voice*, a New York
City weekly newspaper, where she saw a personal ad from
an inmate at a state prison seeking someone to write him.
This intrigued Lori. Although she didn't know what he was
in for, she knew he was lonely and his need touched her
emptiness; and so began a passionate love affair, the first
she had ever known.

"It's been over two years and I feel like a kid. If I don't
see him for two, three days, I get— Then when I know I'm
going to see him, I get so excited. . . . I'm in love. We love
each other. We're crazy about each other."

Lori answered the ad because she was desperately
lonely; Kevin placed the ad for the same reason. Although
they were worlds apart in ages and backgrounds—she's
about fifteen years older—their common need for an emo-

tional connection drew them together. After two letters, Lori visited Kevin.

Kevin was gracious and thoughtful during that first visit. No one had ever treated her that way before. "He was so cute. He got us a little paper towel and he put it down on the table and he put ketchup on my sandwich for me. . . . He was very attentive, which I thought was nice. He wanted to make sure I was comfortable all the time. . . . He asked, 'Are you comfortable in that seat? Would you want me to put your jacket on? Did they give you any problems coming in?' . . . I never saw five hours go so fast in my life."

Of course not. They were, perhaps, the only happy hours Lori had ever had. She didn't yet know about Angela Simon.

ANGELA SIMON

Angela Simon had difficulty socializing. The fifteen-year-old couldn't make small talk about boys, clothes, and music like the other girls could. Angela would walk up to a group of kids and ask for a cigarette as a way of getting into the conversation. She would stand around and smoke, but she didn't talk. "[Angela] was physically attractive but possibly mentally dull," said attorney Sidney Dworet.

Most of the kids in the Islip, Long Island, neighborhood where Angela lived as a foster child teased her. Later, when questioned by officials, these teenagers described Angela as "quiet, introverted, slow intellectually . . . naive and frequently the brunt of ridicule." She was seen a lot on "the path," a shortcut teens used to get to a nearby mall. She also spent time at a local luncheonette, a hangout for neighborhood kids. In Suffolk County police reports, the luncheonette proprietor described Angela as "a good kid, very quiet and reserved . . . who rarely spoke to anyone unless she was spoken to first."

Kevin, during an interview in a prison visiting room, remembered: "She was shy. I felt a protective thing toward her. . . . But I wasn't her boyfriend. She regarded me as a person she could talk to. [The others] picked on her. They teased her."

Angela's favorite refuge was "the hut," an abandoned truck body on the dirt path. The hut was furnished with a blue and white box spring, small filthy scatter rugs, and empty cartons; it was strewn with empty beer cans and cigarette butts. It was not a place that many people knew about, but according to police, a small group of youths, including Angela and Kevin, used the hut as a hangout.

Some of the boys who spent time with Angela in the hut may have been sexually intimate with her, depending on who's telling the story. The boys wrote their nicknames on the walls. They hung out. They wasted time. They sat around drinking beer and smoking cigarettes. On March 18, 1984, one of the boys raped Angela, strangled her, and smashed her head in with a cement block.

THE BIRTHDAY MURDER

According to police in Suffolk County, New York, Kevin celebrated his twenty-first birthday on Sunday, March 18, 1984, by eating a large midday meal with his foster family. Later he went with friends to play video games at the mall. At about five P.M., he met Angela on his way home as he walked along the dirt path. They went into the hut to talk and smoke. Kevin gave her one of his Marlboros. After a while they started to kiss; he felt her breast, then pulled her bra up. When he tried to tug her jeans and underpants down, she resisted and finally, screamed. She tried to get away but he stopped her.

"She continued to resist me and screamed for me to stop," Kevin told police in a taped confession. "I told her she was not going anyplace, that she was staying with me a little longer. I then started to squeeze her neck harder because she wouldn't stop screaming. When she stoped moving, I let her go and took her pants and underpants off. I tried to fuck her, but I couldn't get my dick in her cunt. I checked to see if she was breathing and I knew I killed her.

"To make sure she was dead, I picked up the cement block as high as I could and threw it at Angela's head. . . . I then turned her around on her stomach and put the cement block on her head. I put the box spring across the benches to cover her up." Kevin went home and took a shower. At eight P.M., a friend picked him up and they went bowling to celebrate his birthday.

Kevin's version of his birthday is different from the police version and does not include rape and murder. He said he ate a big dinner in the middle of the day with his Italian foster family as they did every Sunday. After dinner, at about two-thirty P.M., he went to a friend's house and later played video games at the mall. Then he walked back to his house to enjoy a birthday cake. "That's when they think I did it," said Kevin.

That night, he, his friend, and his friend's girl went bowling, then took the girl home. The two guys went drinking; Kevin got drunk on beer, then his friend dropped him off at the local 7-Eleven store. "I knew it was too late for me to go home, so I went to the trailer," said Kevin. His family didn't allow him in if he came home after midnight because he made too much noise, so he decided to sleep in the hut. "I knew there was a mattress there. I thought it was great [that] I wouldn't have to sleep on the floor." In the morning, "I woke up frozen cold and the only thing on my mind was to go home and catch some rest before I would have to go to work." When he later heard Angela Simon's body was found in the hut, he was very upset. "That freaked me out when I heard the girl was underneath the mattress I slept on."

Although Kevin signed a confession, he claims smart, veteran cops coerced him, using the good cop–bad cop tactic to force him to admit to something that wasn't true. "They said, 'If you sign this, you're all right. If you don't sign this, we'll throw away the key.' "

There are great discrepancies between Kevin's story

and police reports, and Kevin continues to maintain his innocence. A brief filed in 1989 in New York Supreme Court's Appellate Division asking for a new trial describes Kevin as "a nervous individual" who was "visibly upset and emotionally unstable" when he was questioned by Suffolk County detectives. The brief maintains that Kevin was questioned in a locked police car in an isolated parking lot, thus violating his constitutional rights, and that no direct evidence was found—blood, hair, fingerprints, etc.—linking him to the murder.

Kevin's defense attorney, Sidney Dworet, interviewed five years after the trial, said: "I didn't defend him believing I was defending a guilty person." But Dworet expressed ambivalence about Kevin's guilt. If he did kill Angela, "he repressed the act into a dream state. . . . He has to deny the act. . . . If he did it, and the evidence seems to indicate that he's done it, his psychology is such that he believes himself to be the kind of person who couldn't hurt anyone."

Added Dworet: "He believes he's innocent. But I'm not certain. . . . He just wants to please everybody. He's a real Eagle Scout. . . . It's hard for me to come to a conclusion there was injustice here. . . . If he didn't do it, where is the murderer now?"

AN EAGLE SCOUT

"To know Kevin, you would know that he couldn't do it. . . . He's too decent of a person. He's never had a record. He's never been in trouble with the law. He was an Eagle Scout. . . . He was a good kid," said Lori. Kevin has lifted her from the tedium of an empty life and she believes in him totally, perhaps more than he believes in himself. He cries when he talks about the murder, but Lori gets angry; she proclaims his innocence, the unfairness of it all, the injustice that this good, kind man is in prison.

Kevin is caring, affectionate, has a good sense of humor, and is ideal for her, according to Lori. He makes her feel happy for the first time in her life. He worries about her well-being and focuses all his attention and affection on her. No one has ever done that for her before, and in gratitude, she promises to remain with Kevin forever. "Love is unselfishness, giving yourself. . . . To be loyal, to stick with the man and not give up on him."

Lori knows Kevin may well lose his appeal and have to spend twenty more years in prison. But she will always believe him to be innocent. "He's just not that sort of person. You have to be a kind of a person to do crimes like that, but he's not." Asked how she would react if she found out he was guilty, Lori has no answer. "I don't know. I would want to know why he did it. I really don't know how I would be able to justify it."

Fortunately, she does not have to make that judgment. To her, Kevin is a victim just as she was throughout her life. They are two hapless souls, clinging together in a lifeboat built of love and need, in a world that is often unjust.

EARLY YEARS

During Lori's empty marriage, her husband "turned aside all the time when I would go to him for affection. . . . He didn't want to be bothered." Once, he told her about a homosexual encounter. "He said this fellow came over and he wanted to do things. . . . And he said he did them and he liked doing them."

Lori was so confused that she used to ask people if what her husband told her was normal. She left him once, but went back because she was emotionally and physically exhausted. Waitressing did not really pay enough to support her.

When Lori was a teenager, she worked after she quit school but turned her paychecks over to her abusive parents. She also took care of the house because her mother was too drunk to bother. "Thinking about it, I must have been like a wife to my father. My mother wasn't around. . . . She was out picking up men, having affairs. . . . My father was working and coming home and sleeping and beating us up. . . . We just lived from day to day. It was survival."

There was rarely anything to eat in the house. More than once, she went without food. Life was hell, and when she got an opportunity to marry, she took it. She met her husband through the church she and her father belonged to until the congregants kicked him out. "We would sit in the parking lot and he'd beat me up in the car. . . . And then a couple of people saw him in bars. . . . Christians don't do that." Although they asked him to leave the church, no one ever reported him for abusing his daughter.

So Lori, eighteen, married the first man she dated. Although she and her husband had intercourse the first night, weeks went by before they again had sex; thus began a pattern that would repeat itself through the marriage. He would ignore her and she would badger him. "I would say, 'Come on, now, we can at least have sex once a week.' Then he made me feel guilty because I had to ask for it. I thought there was something wrong with me because I had been abused."

The unending nightmare of rejection got worse when Lori's father died. He died as he had lived, drunk, in a bar. Lori almost had a breakdown then. "I looked up to this man for so many years, and to know that I had been abused by him . . ." Confused and lost, she turned to her husband for love and affection. She asked him to hold her, to love her, but he refused. "I would just go over and say, 'Put your arms around me. Just, can you hug me?' And he'd say, 'Just get away from me.' "

TRUE LOVE

"I've always been made to feel as though I'm nothing. Being with Kevin, everything was new. It was like I never had a life before. I never had a man treat me like a woman. . . . He called me his princess."

She loves him so much it hurts. At night, she lies in bed, crying, punching the pillow, wishing he were there with his arms around her. When she's unhappy, she tells him; once she talked about suicide. He said, "Oh, God, don't ever say that again." Now, she feels she has something to live for. Even if Kevin's appeal is unsuccessful, they will always have each other.

"I can't believe he's so attentive to me, so considerate. Why me? I'm nobody." This attitude makes Kevin angry; he wants her to have more self-esteem. "He makes me feel as though I'm somebody."

Love is consuming Lori. So new to her, after all these years, it is a feeling she can barely contain. She inhales and exhales love; it radiates from her. She finally has someone who will hold her. In a maximum-security prison waiting room with dozens of people around, he puts his arms around her for five minutes and then asks if it's enough. "No. Just a few minutes longer."

For Lori, whose mother stood on street corners begging money from strangers, whose father raped and beat her, there can never be enough holding.

Although she has difficulty expressing it, Lori feels great rage toward the people who have hurt her. Like so many women, Lori spent her life turning her rage inward, gaining weight, living in misery, depressed all the time. It was not until she met Kevin that she began, with his encouragement, to voice her anger.

"I'm ready to kill somebody." Of course, after she says it, she quickly retracts the angry words. But the power of her rage is frightening.

According to clinical psychologist Stuart Fischoff, Lori may be "trying to rework her past, to finally conquer the unapproachable father" by maintaining a safe relationship with a man behind bars.

But Lori, seeking intimacy with Kevin, is being fooled because their intimacy is an illusion. On the other hand, for the first time in her life Lori is being loved, and there is no underestimating the benefit of that. Her relationship with Kevin is good for her; she knows he cares about her and it makes her feel better about herself. Her life is happier and more fulfilled than it's ever been.

Like other women who love convicted killers, Lori was launched early in her victim career. But victim though she may be, it is clear that, with Kevin's help, she is trying to build up her self-esteem, not tear it down. She has chosen to fall in love with a man who appears to really care about her well-being. When she wrote to him in response to his ad, she chose a person she felt was needy, someone she was certain would answer her letter. Her self-esteem was so low, she assumed no one *but* a lonely inmate would write back.

Kevin gives her love; her husband is still supporting her financially. "At the moment, it's taking two relationships to satisfy her basic needs—without sex, of course," said Dr. Kaye. In a way, Lori is taking care of herself, and this can been seen as a first, positive step. She is actually growing as a result of this relationship and gaining strength from it. Lori believes Kevin to be innocent and is using denial to continue in the relationship.

For Lori, and Kevin, there is a way to forget about being victimized, a way to keep terror away, to prevent real life from intruding into the careful fantasy they are weaving together.

They are like young lovers, sharing an emotion so innocent and pure, it cannot be touched with ugliness or harshness. He is her courtier, all gentleness and sweetness. She is his rescuer, all kind and giving. They remain enclosed in their cocoon of mutual dependence and illusion, separated from real life by more than prison walls.

Devotion

"I work sixty hours a week because I have myself and him to support"

Women who love killers make serious commitments, promising fidelity to men who are locked behind prison walls for the rest of their lives—or at the least, for a very long time. It is a commitment without limit, a devotion that has no bounds. Despite the fact they do not share sexual intimacy, or because of it, their killer/lovers inspire the deepest, most passionate, most committed love in these women. They would never, ever, be unfaithful. Francine said her killer/husband Charlie totally trusts her. "My husband one time told me, 'I'm the only man in prison who doesn't have to worry about his wife, because I know that you don't see other men.' And I don't. . . . For the same reason that I went more than twenty years faithful to my first husband—it would never occur to me to be otherwise."

A man from Huntsville, Texas, doing life for murdering his wife, wrote to me about his fiancé of six years whom he has never met: "Communication, understanding, patience, and a whole lot of love have been the keys to our relationship and its continual growth. . . . Since Cely came into my life, my days are a lot brighter and every day is a good day. . . . How much longer is Cely willing to wait? How ever long it takes. Remember, Cely is Filipino, not American. Filipino women are extremely devoted. In our hearts we are already married."

Despite the men's inaccessibility, women who love men who kill devote their lives obsessively to them. Careers take second place, and the women spend all their savings and extra money on legal fees, sometimes working two jobs to pay for them. Their children are sometimes neglected. They may give up custody of their children, either temporarily or permanently, in order to be near the men they love.

The women put up with incredible hardship. They are alone most of the time; they are financially responsible not only for themselves but for the convicted murderer. Nothing comes easy. Every phone call, every letter, every meeting, means the system has to be dealt with one way or another.

Often, a woman assumes her man's life, his identity; she does his time with him. He's committed the crime but she shares the imprisonment. His legal battle becomes her struggle, his friends and family become her closest allies. In hypothesizing about ending her relationship with a murderer, one woman said it would also mean ending everything else in her life. "I would be giving up a whole lifestyle I have developed. I have become very involved with his family."

Probably the greatest sign of these women's commitment is their patience. They wait—for visits, calls, letters. And of course, they wait for their fantasy to come true: that the man they love, who is on death row or serving a life sentence or life without parole, will eventually be freed, and they will be together.

"I think most people who marry lifers don't believe that he's going to do life in prison," said Ruth, whose husband, Alan, forty, has been in prison for sixteen years. The strength of her fantasy is evident when she refers to the men as "lifers" at the same time that she says most women "don't believe that he's going to do life."

Adds Ruth: "He might do a long time, a very long time, but [everyone] will eventually be parole eligible." This is not true. As of November 1989, eighteen states have sentences of life without parole. And in the cases of particularly heinous mass murders and serial killings, the murderers serve consecutive life sentences (one life sentence after another) for each count of murder, so the likelihood of their being released is nil.

MONEY

"Wives are willing to go out on a limb [for their men]. Mothers tend to be more consistent, but mothers are old and don't have the financial resources," said Alicia. Willingness to commit financially to a murderer is one big proof of loyalty and devotion. Frequently, supporting a murderer in prison forces a woman to work two jobs—and she still has a tough time making ends meet.

"What gets the women I know, long-term, is not the loneliness or the lack of sex or anything else. What wears them down, long-term, is the bills: trying to pay the lawyers, trying to pay the phone bill, trying to support the kids, sending him Christmas boxes. . . . I work sixty hours a week because I have myself and him to support," said Alicia.

These women commit all their money to the men they love. Annette has spent more than $10,000 in legal fees trying to get her husband's murder conviction overturned. He says he's innocent and she believes him. The $10,000 is a bargain, "half-price because the lawyers believe my husband did not do it."

RELOCATION AND CHILDREN

Alicia initially proved her devotion to Bill by leaving her job and her home to relocate to the state where he was imprisoned. She is by no means alone in this; many women who love convicted murderers move to be near the prisons where their men are doing time. In order to be near Jack Henry Abbott, Naomi Zack left her home two hours north of New York City to live near Clinton Maximum Correctional Facility in Dannemora, a few miles from the Canadian border.

Many women also give up their children. When Mary Bain left her husband to be with the man she loved, Joseph Pikul, her daughter remained with her husband. Naomi Zack also left her two children with others when she went to live near Jack Henry Abbott.

When Rochelle fell deeply in love with Duane, she sent her teenage daughter and ten-year-old son to live with their father first, and later with their grandmother. Rochelle also left her home and job and relocated to live near the prison where Duane was serving his sentence.

Sometimes women with grown children wreck their relationships with their offspring because of their obsession with their murderer/lover.

"I turned my whole life around; I loved him. I absolutely adored him," said Elena about Terry, the man she married a few years before he was executed for murder in 1987. Elena had four grown children, three sons and a daughter, when she met Terry, who was about fifteen years younger than she. "My children didn't understand at all and it pretty much broke the bond I had with them. I lived and breathed him, all my waking hours." Elena's daughter "understood quite well," but her sons did not. "They threw a fit and quit speaking to me. . . . They saw themselves cut out by a male person their own age; I would have preferred them to be supportive."

It's surprising that a woman would relinquish her children because of her commitment to a man she has just met and begun to love. But the intensity of the obsessive love felt by women who love killers is incredible. These women have such strong psychological needs that when they think they've really fallen in love, they are willing to give up everything else in their lives for that love—including their children. Nothing can interfere with their love, nothing, not even children.

THE STORY OF RUTH

Ruth, an educated, mature professional woman married to a convicted killer, is eager to talk about commitment. "I want to tell how we managed to survive all the obstacles and made a relationship that we feel meets our needs. . . . I have learned from it. It's been one of the more challenging things in my life and continues to be." Because of her devotion to Alan, she has become director of a local prison-reform advocacy group, an officer of a national prisoners' rights group, and a leading prison rights activist in her state.

Ruth met Alan while she was on a prison tour. They began writing and then "got serious and fell in love," according to a woman who knows Ruth. Alan, convicted of the execution-style slayings of two men in a drug deal sixteen years ago, was a minimum-security inmate because of his good behavior in prison. Ruth and Alan believed their patience was going to pay off when, in the fall of 1989, his sentence was commuted by the governor of the state. The commutation meant he would be able to go before a parole board almost immediately.

But by Christmas, 1989, the governor was under heavy political pressure to reverse the commutation order. Although the State Board of Pardons and Paroles had cited Alan as a rehabilitated model prisoner and had recommended commutation, the governor's actions were viewed as so politically damaging to her and her party, she eventually reversed her decision. Alan is now in a *maximum*-security prison. Officials believe that he is a good candidate for an escape attempt because of his disappointment over the commutation reversal. He is now not eligible for parole until 1999. Ruth remains by his side, and they have publicly said they will appeal the governor's reversal.

Of all the women interviewed for this book, Ruth is by far the closest to accepting the fact that her husband has committed murder. She said, "My husband admits his guilt. He pleaded guilty to first-degree murder. He was too embarrassed to go through a trial. . . . He always took responsibility for being there. He didn't blame his lawyer or anyone else."

However, there are degrees of denial. At one point, Ruth said, "The murder was an aberration as opposed to being part of his criminal activity." Of course. Other than serial killers, who murder as a way of life, all murders are aberrations. Also, she said her husband pleaded guilty to avoid the embarrassment of a trial. But according to a spokesman for the State Department of Corrections, that is not the case. He said Alan pleaded guilty in order to receive a life sentence instead of the death penalty.

Finally, Ruth talked about "degrees of reprehensibility," and one could assume, she meant that the murder of drug dealers is less awful than the murder of innocent people. The families of the murdered men might not agree with her.

STIGMA

Whatever type of murder a man has committed, a woman in love with him often faces the same stigma he does. Society generally believes that a woman who loves a criminal is likely to be a criminal herself. People think a murderer's wife or girlfriend might herself be capable of killing; she is guilty by association and suffers the consequences. Women who love killers, if they tell the truth about their lives, are often ostracized by acquaintances and even by friends and family. Relatives may disown them, refuse to associate with them, and keep them out of the family circle. This makes the women, alienated to start with for many reasons, feel increasingly estranged; they begin to identify more and more with their murderer/lovers.

The women never expect what they have to deal with

in this area. "Nothing they will ever do in their lives, including earning a Ph.D., will prepare them for having a man in prison," said prison-reform activist Jeanette Erickson. "People don't understand. It's never ending: the insults, the injuries, the lies." Not only does society not understand what it's like to love someone who has committed murder, but people don't want to hear about it either. It is expected that a woman with such a "secret" will keep it to herself. Whenever the women interviewed for this book have come out of the closet about their relationships, they have gotten hurt. "You become a target of the neighborhood, a stigma attaches to you as the relative of a murderer," said one woman.

Terry, for example, was on the police force in Galveston, Texas, for four years. She had a steady boyfriend, two children, a good life. Until she met Bobby. Bobby is described by Galveston assistant district attorney George Cooley as "a local drug dealer, burglar, and robber [who] had been in jail three times." Something about Bobby got to Terry; she couldn't resist him. One night while they were at her house the phone rang. It was Terry's ex-boyfriend, Roger. He wanted to come over and talk, and since she had lived with him for so many years, she agreed. When he rang the doorbell, Bobby went into the bedroom. Terry and her ex started to talk, but they quickly became angry and ended up screaming at each other. He punched her in the face. Bobby ran out of the bedroom with a gun—Terry's service revolver. He shot once and Roger fell over, dead.

When the police pulled up to the house minutes later, Terry, crying, hysterical, said that Bobby had murdered her ex-boyfriend. But her story changed by the time a grand jury was convened. Then, Terry testified that Bobby shot in self-defense, that Roger had attacked him first. Terry's son testified also, saying that directly after the shooting, his mother had told him, "Your daddy just killed your daddy."

A grand juror asked Terry what she thought about Bobby, his violence, his quickness to shoot and kill. Terry responded, "I love him and I'm gonna marry him." And she did. Bobby and Terry were married November 3, 1989. She is, of course, no longer a member of the police department.

Cooley voiced the disbelief and shock common to friends and relatives of free women who love murderers. "It's unbelievable to me. She ruined her career. I'm very disappointed with her. . . . I always thought she was a sharp individual. I just can't believe it. . . . He's using her. He's gonna drag her down."

Another woman, a successful professional in a Western state, said, "I may lose my job; my boss is questioning me about my husband." In another state, a leading prison advocate is also afraid publicity surrounding her marriage to a convicted murderer will negatively affect her career.

In Colorado, Annette was suspended from her high school teaching job because of public reaction to accusations against her by prison officials. These officials barred Annette from visiting her husband, Jack, a convicted murderer, saying she "had been seen fondling [him] during a visit," according to *The Rocky Mountain News*. A year later, after a long battle to vindicate herself, officials at the prison apologized and Annette was once again allowed to visit Jack. (She had not seen her husband for a year!) She was also rehired by her school district and given back pay.

There is no limit to the humiliation women who love killers must undergo when they visit their men. One woman, whose husband is in a Massachusetts prison doing time for murder, said that visiting wives and girlfriends have to change their tampons in front of a female prison guard. Prison officials know that contraband is smuggled in, are aware of the methods used, and generally expect wives and girlfriends to do the smuggling.

"Visitors are treated like dogs," said Hilary. "If you have a metal clip on your bra, you have to remove your bra. If I bring pictures of the grandkids in, they look at them to make sure they're not pornography."

Lori said, "It is humiliating. You're being incarcerated right along with them. The way [the guards] look at you, like you're a third-class citizen coming through, like you're the scum of the earth."

Tricia Hedin, a prison activist from Oregon, has had a baby with her inmate husband through artificial insemination. In *Newsweek,* she wrote: "One day, in the visiting room, I see a woman's hand slapped by a prison guard when she places it on her husband's knee. Another day, another woman is kept waiting for half of her three-hour visit as prison officials try to 'find' her husband and bring him to the visiting room."

Said Alicia, "I have one foot on the inside and one foot on the outside and am straddling the wall. We don't live in the free world. We sit home nights by ourselves because we can't get involved with someone else because we're involved with someone—but that someone you have isn't there with you. He can't be with you. The inmates don't realize how much this dominates your life."

Women Who Love Serial Killers

"I got me a good one"

Ted Bundy murdered thirty-one women and girls in four states. "Hillside Stranglers" Kenneth Bianchi and Angelo Buono killed ten women. John Wayne Gacy strangled thirty-three young men and boys. In California, "Night Stalker" Richard Ramirez killed fourteen people. David Berkowitz, "Son of Sam," shot six people in New York City.

Incredibly, every one of these multiple killers, whose crimes were bizarre, repulsive, and inhuman, has had at least one woman fall in love with him. Three of the six men were married after being convicted as murderers.

Bundy, executed in 1989, married Carole Boone, whom he met during his trial; she bore him a son. Bianchi married a Louisiana woman, Shirlee Book, in 1989. Buono remarried one of his former wives while he was in prison. Gacy's former girlfriend, Sue Terry, told the world in television and newspaper interviews that she was passionately in love with him. Richard Ramirez's fans—women who correspond with him and followed him faithfully from courtroom to jail—fantasize they love him. David Berkowitz has had at least one girlfriend and is now supposedly in another relationship.

Who are these women? Do they differ from other women who love murderers? How do women who love serial killers deny the hideous crimes committed by the men they believe they love?

WOMEN WHO LOVE SERIAL KILLERS

"Particularly notorious inmates attract prison groupies. . . . [Serial killers are] more famous, more prominent, more sinister, more recognition enhancing" than ordinary killers, said psychiatrist Park Dietz. Relationships with these men can give women social significance, perhaps for the first time in their lives.

Serial killers provide themselves with a "celebrity career . . . The public treats them as major celebrities. . . . Virtually all our multiple murderers achieve true and lasting fame. They thus attain an immortality denied the unenterprising common man," writes Elliot Leyton in *Hunting Humans*.

Some women's fascination with serial killers is "the most excessive hero worship and passion that I have ever encountered," said Leyton. The glamour and celebrity status given these killers creates an escalating excitement. When the bodies are found, there is a kind of a prearrest celebrity; once the killer is caught, he becomes a genuine celebrity with a sensational kind of allure.

Women who love serial killers, not unlike women who love men who have killed once or twice, are attracted by notoriety. In our hierarchy of criminal celebrity, the serial killer is at the top, so his status gives his woman a boost, playing on her quite common and universal desire to become known. "If you can't get your fifteen minutes of fame, you can get close to someone who got it. If he raped and killed, that doesn't matter so much," said psychologist Jonathan Segal, Ph.D. When an individual develops a romantic interest in a celebrity to the point of pursuing that celebrity, he or she may be suffering from a psychological condition called erotomania. The pursuers are often "plucked from . . . obscurity" by contact, real or imagined, with the celebrity, wrote Segal in "Erotomania Revisited."

MACHISMO

Of course, there is a dark side to women's romantic feelings for serial killers. Even if she insists on his innocence, somewhere inside her, she knows she loves a brutal killer, and often, a violator of women. And somewhere inside her, she is excited by this knowledge.

"In a twisted kind of way, the male who is the most strong and dominant—and most violent—will appear to be the most male," said Leyton. The serial killer takes on a maleness that is attractive to women who, because of the limitations of their psyches, can't see the difference between real strength and brute violence.

Story after story of the appeal of the serial killers for women illustrates this. "Outside the courtroom, some of them [the Ted groupies] would admit to reporters that Ted frightened them, yet they couldn't stay away. It is a common syndrome, this fascination that an alleged mass killer has for some women, as if he was the ultimate macho figure," wrote Ann Rule in *The Stranger Beside Me,* about Ted Bundy.

TED BUNDY

During his four-year coast-to-coast killing rampage, Ted Bundy kidnapped, tortured, raped, and murdered thirty young women and at least one child. One expert on serial killers believes the total to be much higher. Bundy may have committed more than one hundred murders, according to Robert Keppel, chief investigator for Washington State's Attorney General's Office. No one is positive how many states Bundy killed in—four, five, six—or more. After a lengthy investigation, trial, and appeal period, Bundy, convicted of three of the murders, was executed in Florida on January 24, 1989.

Despite being apprehended by the authorities, Bundy's career was not over. Although the murders would stop, his celebrity career was just starting, and his notoriety would draw countless women to him. For the duration of his trial and imprisonment, Bundy had a huge following. "A lot of believers in him thought that he wasn't the killer. A lot of people were stuck on his good looks, upper-middle-class attitude, being the aspiring attorney, going to school," said Keppel.

During Bundy's trial, "one front row was somehow reserved for the Ted Groupies . . . The front row—just behind Ted and the defense team—was jammed with pretty young women. . . . Their eyes never left Ted, and they blushed and giggled with delight when he turned to flash a blinding smile at them, as he often did," wrote Ann Rule in *The Stranger Beside Me.* "Handsome, arrogant and articulate, he drew scores of rapt groupies to the jammed court each day," wrote Stephen G. Michaud and Hugh Aynesworth in *The Only Living Witness.* The women, some young, some older, were all eager to see in person the "Love-Bite Killer," as the newspapers had dubbed Bundy.

Some of Bundy's courtroom worshipers "sent him lewdly suggestive notes or asked for his autograph. Others were content to sit for a full day in court, happy if just once he would look their way," wrote Michaud and Aynesworth, adding that he had a "national following" and received "heavy fan mail."

Who were these women? How could they love a creature called Ted Bundy?

One Ted groupie contacted anthropologist and writer Elliott Leyton because she saw him on television in 1986 promoting his book *Hunting Humans.* After the show, he was told he had an urgent phone call. The woman at the other end of the line said she was desperately in love with Bundy. "She asked did I think he really did it. I said that there was no question in my mind. But that didn't seem to deter her," said Leyton.

In her letters to Leyton "she admitted that she had an uncontrollable passion for Bundy," he recalled. The woman was single, in her late twenties or early thirties, and worked in a hotel in Toronto. Although she had never met the serial killer, she told Leyton she couldn't stop thinking about him, that she was "obsessively involved in a kind of romantic fantasy about Bundy." She stopped writing after a few months and Leyton never heard from her again.

Bundy was incarcerated at Florida State Penitentiary during the decade between his death sentences and his execution. Prison administrator Paul Decker said he had never seen an inmate with as many groupies as Bundy, "a variety of women . . . [Bundy had] quite a number of personal relationships with women."

All through Bundy's trials and years of appeals, "he would always have at least one woman entranced with him, living for the few moments she could visit him in jail, running errands, proclaiming his innocence," writes Rule. The most steadfast, Carole Ann Boone, married him and had his child.

Like other women in love with killers, Carole needed and wanted love so much that she created a fantasy lover whom she named "Bunny." Also, because Bundy was a serial killer, his notoriety gave Boone status. She was not a nobody anymore but Ted Bundy's wife. Her opinions, ideas, life story, feelings—she, Carole Ann Boone, was a magnet for hundreds of reporters from all over the world.

Like other women who love murderers, Boone gave up everything in her life for her man. She relocated from Seattle to Gainesville, Florida, to be near him, taking her son from a previous relationship with her. When Boone went public about their relationship, she lost her county clerical job and had to subsist on whatever reporters were willing to pay her for interviews. She became Bundy's voice in the outside world. From the moment they connected, she was a true believer, utterly convinced of his innocence. She had to be, in order to maintain her fantasy. She worked tirelessly, albeit unsuccessfully, to prove the charges against him false. Boone spent years being enraged at the press, the prosecution, the legal system—the forces in society that had ganged up on her poor, innocent Bunny.

Finally, as Ted Bundy stood charged with dozens of heinous murders and was facing death, as he was described in the media as one of the most vicious sexual sadists and serial killers ever, Carole Ann Boone married him. While acting as his own defense attorney, Bundy got Carole on the stand and asked her if she wanted to wed him. She replied, "Yes," and he said, "Then I do hereby marry you." Although the method was unconventional, it was legal, and the two would remain bonded in unholy matrimony until Bundy's execution.

Like the Toronto woman who was obsessed with Bundy, Carole did not love Ted Bundy, the man, because he didn't reveal himself to her, or to anyone. She loved Bunny, her own creation, what she wanted him to be—not what he was.

Sitting through Bundy's trial, Carole Boone managed to believe in the innocence of her fantasy lover because the side of himself that Bundy showed was charming and courteous; he could not possibly be a serial killer. Boone's ability to deny was shored up by Bundy's incredible lies. "He hoodwinked Carole to the extent that she believed he didn't do it despite what the evidence showed," said Investigator Keppel. Two years before Bundy's execution, Carole Boone stopped believing in her husband's innocence and stopped visiting him.

Journalist Richard Larsen, author of *Ted Bundy: The Deliberate Stranger,* a man who knew Bundy in Washington long before his arrest, speculated on why Carole Boone stopped believing in her Bunny. "She didn't really tell me, but probably a good conclusion is the accumulation of circumstance, circumstance, circumstance. Probably the events in the sorority murders, the fact that Ted was living adjacent to the sorority house, that the police description resembled him, and the rather powerful set of circumstances [surrounding the murder] of the twelve-year-old girl. These were the cappers of her conclusion."

Although all these facts were brought out during Bundy's trial, it took eight years for Carole Boone to believe they were true.

The FBI agent who spent the last five days of Bundy's life with him said that, even then, the serial killer did not lack the company of women. "One of his lady attorneys started seeing him regularly," said Special Agent William Hagmaier III.

Attorney Diana Weiner, who represented Bundy in civil matters, was described in the *Sarasota Herald Tribune* as knowing a Ted Bundy who was quite different from the serial killer the public knew: "While emphasizing that she isn't trying to minimize the heinous acts Bundy committed, Weiner says she believes Bundy was genuine in expressing remorse and sensitivity toward others."

According to the article, Weiner said, "I think the public is unwilling to accept that there could be a commonality between Ted Bundy and the rest of humanity or that Ted Bundy could have, at the end of his life, sought to tell the truth, confess or have any moral compunction to do so."

Could Weiner have fallen under the charismatic killer's spell? "He has inspired passionate love and hopeless love," write Michaud and Aynesworth, adding that Bundy's psychopathology was what he used to "bind women to him." Put another way, he was the consummate sociopath. The cons he used for tricking women into getting into his car so he could then sexually brutalize and kill them were the same cons he used on the women who "loved" him.

JOHN WAYNE GACY

On death row in Illinois, John Wayne Gacy has been waiting to die since 1980 for the hideous sexual murders of thirty-three youths. The epitome of the serial killer who blends into the background, Gacy was a jovial, outgoing, friendly man, considered sociable and charitable. He organized town parades and dressed as a clown to cheer up sick children in the local hospital. Once nominated "Man of the Year" by the Jaycees of Springfield, Illinois, he was even photographed with former first lady Rosalynn Carter at a local political rally.

He lived in a quiet Chicago suburb and was married twice, fathering two children with his first wife, Marlynn. During his second marriage, to Carol, he began his killings. They lasted for a period of about six years, between 1972 and 1978. At the beginning of 1975, as he and Carol were divorcing, Gacy's drinking, pill-taking, and murders escalated. Neither of Gacy's wives, nor his neighbors, friends, or acquaintances, had the remotest idea of the monster he really was.

Today, more than a decade later, Gacy still denies he is a serial killer. His claim is that journalists have painted an inaccurate portrait of him. In many of his letters quoted in *They Call Him Mr. Gacy,* a collection of his correspondence, he repeats this line: "There is a great deal of difference between John Gacy, the man, and John Gacy, the Media monster."

They Call Him Mr. Gacy is replete with letters from women desperate to meet a sadistic serial killer. The writers show evidence of unhappy marriages, traumatic experiences, deviance—and above all, loneliness. Most of the women express sympathy for Gacy and a belief in his innocence. Their letters are full of the denials and fantasies we have seen expressed by all women who love murderers.

From Randi, Maine, August 13, 1984: "I have this obsession with you. I can't for the life of me stop thinking about you. . . . I would like to meet you someday. . . . I would like to get to know about you personally. I don't think, to tell you the truth, you got a fair trial. . . . I would like to have you as a friend; I live in these back woods with my parents and it gets awfully lonely."

From Lynn, New York City, November 28, 1987: "I was an attractive girl who got scarred through some fault of her own and now live as a recluse. I only like to know people who have crossed over to the other side. I am still healthy and feel beautiful in a very rough hewn sort of way but I can't relate to most normal things or situations. I create companions out of my dolls and work on a phone S&M service (at home) so I'm able to keep my worldly interaction limited. I am a mental stimulation junkie—need to read or watch movies all the time. Roller skate in my apartment for hours to ease frustrations. Have a dog who I jerk off . . . I wonder about you and where you've been."

From Carolyn, Centralia, Illinois, June 12, 1980: "My marriage took me down but I'm coming up slow but sure. *Ha.* Do you ever have visitors? I feel sorry for you and I hope everything works out!"

From Terry-Sue, March 2, 1988: "I am a 34 year old black sexy mama. I am looking for a swinging good time whenever you get out. I know you killed them boys but I don't care. . . . P.S. This is a train letter. Please send it to the rest of you killer friends."

From Kerri, Milwaukee, March 3, 1988: "I've just got over a bad relationship with my x-boyfriend. He was a real bitch—but rather exciting. We would have these wild fights where we would hit each other, scream at the top of our lungs. John I got 'great lungs.' Wait til you see—perhaps by photo."

From Nancy, Phoenix, Arizona, March 22, 1988: "I wish to express my sorrow for the many years you have spent in prison and on death row. I have from the very beginning believed in your innocence, and still do till this day."

From Wanetta, on January 28, 1989: "I am aware that you might not choose to answer my letter, that will be a great loss for me to have the chance to confer with the infamous John Gacy, would be a great honor to someone like me who finds you one of the most intelligent murderers of our time."

Gacy is not handsome, youthful, or charismatic. He doesn't have Bundy's appeal to women nor did he have avid fans and groupies following his case. He has, however, achieved celebrity status. And the abundance of letters he gets from strangers, women he has never met or contacted, shows how many lonely, deluded women out there want contact with a notorious killer—either to become notorious themselves or perhaps because they're attracted by his deviance.

Of the many women who tried to meet Gacy, perhaps the most successful was an Illinois mother of eight, Sue Terry, who first wrote to Gacy after reading about him in a newspaper. Instead of being repulsed by Gacy's crimes, Sue felt empathy. Herself a victim, she saw in Gacy a fellow sufferer—common to many women who love men who kill. "I thought maybe he is in prison because someone had made a mistake. I thought he might be innocent," she said.

Although he responded to her letter as if he didn't trust her, she went to visit him anyway. Sue was "shocked" when she met Gacy. "He's got real soft, kind blue eyes. He relaxed me, the way he talked. I can't explain it. It was like being in another world," she said. The forty-six-year-old woman visited the serial killer constantly for a year. They also wrote to each other every day and talked on the phone, according to Sue. "I was in love with him. . . . I never had anybody treat me as nice as he treated me." For Sue Terry, who describes her life as "hard and rough," who experienced a series of abusive relationships, unwanted pregnancies, and feelings of victimization, John Wayne Gacy was the first person she ever met who acted as if he cared.

Using denial and compartmentalization, Sue was able to avoid the truth about Gacy so she could view him as a kind, considerate man and fall in love with him. "I really and truly believed he was innocent. How could people do this to John? He was the nicest, kindest, sweetest person in the world. . . . It wouldn't be the John I know to do something like that."

Like so many women who love men who kill, Sue grew up in a home without a father; he'd abandoned the family when she was two. "I had a mother and [step]dad who cared about me, but for some reason, my brothers were the main thing in [my mother's] life." At fourteen, after an affair with a married man, Sue gave birth to her first baby. Pregnant again a few years later, she found herself still single when her boyfriend died in a car accident. Next, she had two children with "a man who really cared about me and loved me, but I never really loved him in that way. . . . I was depressed."

The relationship she had right before she met Gacy was the worst of her life. She lived for five years with a violently abusive man who tortured her: "He cut the ends of my fingers off, bone and all. He beat me so bad. . . . Me and my kids slept in cars, did anything to get away from him. He kicked my teeth out and cut my face. . . . [I needed] over one hundred stitches.

"I see this on television, where women kill their husbands. If I could have, I would have. I would be in prison now for murder."

Finally, Sue managed to leave her tormentor and until she met Gacy, had nothing to do with men. But Gacy was different from other men. He had killed, over and over; he had committed the crime Sue could only talk about. Much of Sue's attraction to Gacy has to do with his ability to act while she could only threaten or imagine (like Maria in Chapter 1). Even though she denied his guilt, somewhere inside Sue knew he had really murdered the thirty-three boys and young men.

Sue and Gacy were close for about a year until he bragged so much about his murders, she could no longer maintain her illusions about his innocence. It's difficult for a woman in love with a murderer to deny his guilt if he admits it. Once, when Sue took her children to prison to visit Gacy, her son said he had heard of a serial killer with more victims. Gacy became angry. "It made him mad to think someone had killed more than he did. He said, 'No, he didn't. I killed more than he did.' . . . I had seen the cold, mean side of John Wayne Gacy." Another time, referring to his victims, he told Sue, "All those boys were prostitutes."

Today, only Sue's sixteen-year-old daughter believes

Gacy to be innocent. "He still writes to my little girl. . . . She just kind of feels sorry for him. He's got her believing now that if he dies, they killed an innocent man. She doesn't think he's guilty."

Gacy conned Sue into believing he was wrongly convicted just as he is now tricking her daughter. "He is the world's greatest manipulator. I don't know how, but believe me, he just does it. . . . He could con a snake."

THE HILLSIDE STRANGLERS: KENNETH BIANCHI AND ANGELO BUONO

Kenneth Bianchi looked up to his older cousin, Angelo Buono. When the younger man moved from his home in Rochester, New York, to L.A. at the age of twenty-six, he and his cousin began to pal around. Buono, forty-four, was a street-smart, macho kind of guy who "lived with a strict code," according to Gerald Chaleff, Buono's defense attorney. Buono married three times, had seven children, and was a self-employed car upholsterer. He was also a known troublemaker, thief, and bully whose children called him The Buzzard. Buono did not have any charm; he was the darker, grimmer side of the killing duo.

Bianchi "is the consummate con man, always got something going on in his mind, always trying to set something up. [He has] above-average intelligence, a gift for gab, and he's good-looking, according to some women," said Sgt. Frank Salerno of the L.A. Sheriff's Department, one of the principal investigators on the Hillside Strangler case.

Although the two men were very different, they had enough in common to allow them to kill as a single unit. Both saw women as objects to be discarded when their usefulness was over. Both liked to torture and kill women for kicks. They observed the machismo rule of the streets: men dominate, women are dominated.

"Bianchi loved to kill and he was crazy. Buono just

kind of manipulated the whole thing. If a girl didn't do what she was supposed to, they would just kill her," said social worker Lois Lee.

During a five-month period between October 1977 and February 1978, the cousins raped, tortured, and strangled ten young women and girls. They gassed some victims, injected cleaning solution into others, burned a few, and sexually brutalized all. Their two youngest victims were twelve and fourteen. They dumped the bodies like so much garbage on hillsides in Los Angeles.

It wasn't until Bianchi murdered again in Washington State that the cousins were apprehended. Bianchi, ordered to leave L.A. by Buono to let things cool down, moved to Bellingham, Washington, but after a while, he felt the urge to murder. Killing was his work and he didn't feel good unless he was working. In January 1979, Bianchi strangled two college girls to death.

Caught when police became aware of similarities in the Bellingham murders and the unsolved Hillside Stranglings, Bianchi tried a variety of ruses to get himself off. He constructed an elaborate scheme—which almost succeeded—in which he pretended that he had multiple personalities. Some psychiatrists bought his act, but others didn't. He was finally deemed to be sane—or sane enough to accept the consequences of his acts under the law.

As did Bundy and Gacy in their communities, Bianchi lived as a model citizen in Bellingham. He even had a girlfriend with whom he had a son. "The arrest of Kenneth Bianchi on suspicion of murder was a surprise to everyone in Bellingham who had known him. Kelli Boyd, Ken's girlfriend and the mother of his baby, always thought of him as a gentle man who was kind to her and to his friends," wrote Jack Levin and James Alan Fox in *Mass Murder: America's Growing Menace.*

When police presented Bianchi with evidence of his guilt and refused to believe his multiple-personality hype, he decided to accept a deal. He would plead guilty to the

Washington murders and to five of the California killings and would also testify against his cousin. In return, he would receive a life sentence instead of the death penalty.

When Angelo Buono's trial finally got under way in Los Angeles, prosecutors were afraid they would fail to convict him because of insufficient evidence and because much of their case rested on the testimony of the obviously unstable Bianchi. They asked to have the charges against Buono dropped. But Judge Ronald George refused to honor the prosecutors' request and the trial proceeded; after two years, Buono was convicted of nine murders. He was sentenced to life without parole, even though the jury had the option of sentencing him to death.

Both Kenneth Bianchi and Angelo Buono, convicted and in prison for life, are, or have been, married men. Their victims are long dead, and the families of those victims have suffered incredible trauma and loss. But the killers have been allowed to marry, and each enjoys the comfort, warmth, and affection of a woman who loves him. And while their victims' names have faded into oblivion, Bianchi and Buono are still celebrities.

When Kenneth Bianchi married Shirlee Book on September 21, 1989, news of the wedding was flashed over the Associated Press wire service. The thirty-six-year-old Louisiana woman's romance began when she wrote to Bianchi, now thirty-eight, after she saw a picture of him looking lonely during his trial. On television's "Hard Copy," Shirlee described her husband as "affectionate, loving." On the same show, Bianchi says, "I killed those broads."

According to a neighbor who spoke with Diane Albright, a reporter, at one time Shirlee tried to become romantically involved with Ted Bundy, but apparently he wasn't interested and she moved on to Bianchi. "She's always writing to prisons. She wrote to Ted Bundy, to several prisoners. She reads a lot and her house is filled with books about killers and serial killers," said the neighbor.

Richard Bauer, assistant superintendent at Washington State Penitentiary where Bianchi is serving his sentence, described Shirlee as "very timid and a plain-looking lady with reddish-brown hair, about five feet five inches." Shirlee never believed that Ted Bundy was a serial killer. She told Albright, "They killed him, an innocent man. They weren't Christians who done that to him." Book—who never had a relationship with Bundy—said, "I would still be with him if they hadn't fried him."

During the three years that Shirlee and Bianchi corresponded, she expressed her fantasies in letters—her dreams, what she wanted out of life, what their life would be like once he got out of prison. Intent on marrying Bianchi although they had not yet met, Shirlee bought a trousseau and a fancy white wedding gown and sent wedding invitations.

Shirlee Book married serial killer Kenneth Bianchi wearing floor-length white satin, a veil, and white gloves. The couple expected to receive conjugal visits, but Washington State Penitentiary denied their request. Shirlee was very happy. "His future is bright. He'll be a free man and it won't be long," she told Albright. "I got me a good one."

It's possible that to Shirlee Book, who like Sue Terry has had a hard life, marriage to Kenneth Bianchi represents a way out because of his notoriety and celebrity. Shirlee's first husband, Billy, with whom she had a son when she was seventeen, "was as crazy as she was. They would take nerve pills and things like that. He was kind of mental. He drank cleaning or lighter fluid after they split up," said neighbor Betty Day. After this marriage, Shirlee became involved with a much younger man. "He treated her okay, but he stole things. . . . He was in trouble with the law."

Shirlee is extremely close to her mother. Day described a family in which the father did all the caretaking at home, including housework, because Shirlee and her mother are not functional much of the time. "Shirlee stays up all night and sleeps all day; she's temperamental. She'll rant and rave all night and then take pills to sleep all day," said Day. Shirlee "has always been interested in notorious people" but does not now grant interviews because Bianchi won't allow her to. Since the Book family has no telephone, many of

Shirlee's conversations with Bianchi are made on Day's phone. Day believes that Bianchi, thousands of miles away and imprisoned, controls his wife. "He won't let her give interviews. Kenneth won't let her. What I really believe is he wants control over her. If she talks to people and makes any money, then he won't control her."

Sgt. Frank Salerno said that Bianchi can only relate to unattractive women he can dominate and control. Shirlee reportedly has no teeth and is extremely thin. "The fact that she is unattractive does fit with Bianchi. Most of his close relationships were with women who were maybe homely or overweight. . . . The woman who mothered his child, Kelli Boyd, was overweight during their relationship. . . . But the women Bianchi attacked were attractive and well built," said Salerno.

Both Shirlee Book and Sue Terry are attracted to the serial killers they love for their notoriety. And even while these women deny that the men they love are guilty, they are exploiting the situation—making appearances on television and granting interviews for books and articles. Shirlee and Sue are also attracted to violence. These women may not be able to go out and commit murder themselves, but they have had murderous thoughts and fantasies. Erroneously equating power with violence and strength with cruelty, they live vicariously through their killer/lovers and feel, just for a moment, that they, too, are strong and powerful.

The other Hillside Strangler, Angelo Buono, remarried a woman he divorced years earlier, according to Lt. Cammy Voss, spokeswoman at Folsom Prison. They have since been divorced again, she said. He has also had at least one other woman interested in him who moved from southern California to be near the prison where he is incarcerated, said Sgt. Frank Salerno. Right now, Buono is not married or involved with any woman, but it's probably only a matter of time before some woman on the outside starts feeling sorry for him and ends up in love.

DAVID BERKOWITZ, THE SON OF SAM

In New York City in 1976, David Berkowitz shot eight people; six died and two were paralyzed. His random, serial attacks, usually against young women sitting with their dates in parked cars, gave New York the feeling of a city under siege. Many residents recall being too terrified to leave their apartments.

Since he shot his victims instead of strangling them, Berkowitz didn't have the twisted machismo of a Buono or a Bundy, but appealed more to the nurturing, maternal side of women. Maury Terry, author of *The Ultimate Evil,* recalled that Berkowitz received numerous letters from women after his arrest in August 1977. "They wrote, 'I think you're sexy and handsome and misunderstood.' One signed her letter, 'David's girl,' " said Terry. The letters focused on his blue eyes and his innocence.

David Abrahamsen, M.D., the psychiatrist who testified that Berkowitz was competent to stand trial, said Berkowitz had a woman in love with him. The woman knew Berkowitz before he was arrested and stood by him after his conviction, making the tedious bus trip from New York City to Dannemora Correctional Facility near the Canadian border every three weeks for seven years, from 1977 to 1985, according to Maury Terry. "There, in the motel where she stayed, she would act like Greta Garbo because her boyfriend was Son of Sam—like she could get whatever she wanted, like she was important," said the writer. Although this woman wanted to marry Berkowitz, the relationship didn't work out. He's now incarcerated in New York State's Sullivan Correctional Facility, and a fellow inmate has said Berkowitz has a new girlfriend.

MASS MURDERERS

In addition to serial killers, the FBI's National Center for the Analysis of Violent Crime also studies mass murderers, defined as those who kill four or more victims at one location within one event. Spree killings are murders at two or more locations with no cooling-off time in between. From 1977 to November 1989, the FBI Academy library reports 112 known mass murderers who are responsible for killing 657 people, and 50 known spree killers who murdered 306 people. Mass murderers are more likely than serial killers to commit suicide after they've taken their victims' lives.

One such killer, Ramon Salcido, lives on. And he lives on in a relationship with a loving, supportive woman who believes in him.

On April 14, 1989, in California's Sonoma Valley, Salcido wiped out seven people: his twenty-three-year-old wife, Angela; two of his three daughters, Sofia, four, and Teresa, one; his mother-in-law; and his wife's two young sisters, ages twelve and eight. He also ambushed and shot to death the assistant manager at Grand Cru Winery where he worked. Salcido unsuccessfully tried to murder two more people: a supervisor at the winery and his third child, Carmina, three. Salcido, from jail, is battling his wife's father for custody of Carmina; he wants his family to have her.

Salcido's girlfriend, Barbara Pater, is loyal, loving, and faithful. "She wants to marry him. She says, 'I love this man.' She's young, fairly attractive. She looked like she may be normal. She is in love with him, saying he couldn't have done these things," said Lt. Cammy Voss at Folsom Prison. At the Sonoma County Jail, a spokesman for the county sheriff's department said Pater began showing up in court in May 1989 during Salcido's preliminary hearings. Pater said she was interested in helping people and has seen Salcido once or twice a week since, although he's under tight security and the couple is separated by a glass wall during visits. Pater, described as almost thirty, lists her occupation as "finder of lost people." After she began her relationship with Salcido, she moved from southern California to live in Sonoma County to be near him.

On December 17, 1990, Salcido was sentenced to die in the San Quentin gas chamber for the six murders he committed.

Conclusion: Beyond the Walls

"We might not even like each other in the real world"

Women who love killers were often little girls lost, reared in dysfunctional families where they were victims of abuse at the hands of harsh, dictatorial fathers aided by passive mothers. A large percentage were raised as Catholics and were severely affected by oppressive church teachings, including sexism, subjugation of women, and repression of sexuality.

Fathers were missing: divorced, dead, always working, drunk, withdrawn. Occasionally, mothers took on father's role and behaved like demanding authoritarians. Women who love killers frequently found that their relationships with men mimicked the one they had with their fathers. Married young, their first husbands were often violent, alcoholic, sexually and/or emotionally abusive.

Although the women interviewed say they were not looking for love when they met the convicted murderers they eventually fell for, all the women were somehow drawn to this population of society's outcasts. Writing letters through

pen pal programs, answering ads, volunteering, working—
they all managed to meet a convicted killer one way or
another. "Love" grew quickly in prison visiting rooms, and
against her will, each woman was soon obsessed with her
beloved/murderer.

IS IT LOVE?

As it was between medieval maidens and the courtly knights
who protected them, sex and true intimacy between women
and the killers they love is usually forbidden by prison systems. These women feel deeply, but what they feel is not
mature love or adult sexual passion. It is *romantic* passion—
a passion fueled by deprivation and suffering, enhanced by
anguish. These women have found the key to never-ending
romance: suffering and pain.

    Because many women who love killers have real diffi-
culties with intimacy because of the damage done to them
in childhood, they have chosen to live a fantasy. The majority
of these women don't love real men but an illusion that is
based on denial. Each woman separates, or compartmentalizes, the murder from the man she loves. She denies his
crime.

    For women who love serial killers, or other notorious
murderers, there is the added thrill of fame. Each serial
killer's status gives a woman with low self-esteem a sense of
importance; her prestige rises in direct proportion with the
heinousness of his crimes.

KILLERS: THE MOST MACHO MEN

In our patriarchal culture, murderers are often viewed as
more than male: the most macho, strong, violent, and brutal
of all men. In a majority of movies and television shows, the
violent mystique of the murderer—or the cop, spy, under-
cover agent, etc.—is the erotic centerpiece. Murderers "rep-

resent the most profound, extreme kind of fear . . . They become culture heroes and are portrayed as very erotic. In a patriarchal culture, in a male supremacist culture, violence itself is eroticized. The murder itself becomes an erotic art," said feminist theorist Dr. Jane Caputi. Murder becomes sexy so a murderer becomes a superstud.

For some women, it *is* thrilling to dance with a master of death. If a woman is seeking excitement, passion, a meaning to life, loving a murderer can make her feel intensely alive. She becomes important, perhaps famous, because she loves a man who has killed.

As we have seen, many of these women take orders from their boyfriends or husbands even though the men are behind bars. Criminologist and author Dr. James Fox visited convicted serial killer Douglas Clark (the Sunset Slayer) and his wife, Kelly: "He's very controlling. In the visiting room, he'll smoke a cigarette and the smoke will get in her eyes. She'll put up with it for a while. Then she'll get up to put the cigarette out. By the time she gets back [from walking to the ashtray], he'll have another one lit." The couple, married for five years, met after Clark was convicted of the sexually sadistic murders of several women in L.A. "Kelly thinks he's innocent; she wants to prove his innocence, free him," said Dr. Fox. But, he added, if Clark should ever be freed, their relationship would not endure: "He'd be gone."

A murderer is often a con man who wins a woman by manipulation and lying. Some women, gullible, vulnerable, and needy, are ready to believe these charmers. Each women hears a story that fits her needs: If she needs to believe that he's religious, he'll tell her that. If she wants sweet talk, he'll woo her. If she needs a brilliant existential hero, he'll sweep her off her feet with his verbiage. Some murderers are unbelievably charismatic. These men exude self-confidence. The narcissistic and antisocial personalities of these murderers cause them to act as though rules don't apply to them. They act tough and superior. They believe in themselves (or pretend they do) and easily convince susceptible women (little girls lost) to believe in them also. But in truth, these are deeply disturbed men who, by murdering, have irrevocably broken one of our most basic laws.

Having killed and been caught and imprisoned, would they kill again? Most people believe so, but to women in love with killers, women who deny the crime, the answer is definitely no. My man is rehabilitated, says each woman. Moreover, he is gentle, intelligent, sensitive. Kill again? He is no more likely to kill than you or I, she says.

Every relationship between a woman and a killer is based on the hope he will be freed. At the same time that she denies his crime, she also believes he is rehabilitated. He will never do anything like that again, she thinks. I will work, I will sacrifice, I will do whatever I have to in order to secure his release so we can live happily ever after . . . beyond the walls.

BEYOND THE WALLS

Sometimes the dream shared by these women, that their men will be freed, does come true. A murderer is paroled, released, or pardoned, and he and the woman who loves him— who has sacrificed for him and fought like a mother bear protecting her cubs to secure his release—can walk off together into paradise. But how often does this happen? Of the women interviewed for this book, only one had succeeded in reaching nirvana with her freed killer/lover. The majority of men remain imprisoned no matter how impassioned the fight for their freedom. And the women who love them remain beside them, giving, nurturing, supporting, sacrificing, denying.

Each woman in love with a convicted killer fantasizes that on that day which is her entire focus, her reason for being, the day he walks out of prison a free man, they will begin to share a life of unending romance, undying love— with no intrusion of reality, such as bills, kids, and laundry.

The problem with this dream is that convicted murderers are unlikely to be released. We know that some are paroled—sometimes to kill again, such as Shawcross in Rochester, New York—but generally, nothing ever materializes for these men. There is no parole for serial killer Kenneth Bianchi, no new trial for Duane, no pardons for Alan or Charlie. In short, only failure and frustration for these dreamers, men and women alike.

Occasionally, a woman in love with a killer will make an interesting assessment of what life after prison would be like. Maria (Chapter 1) told television interviewer Sally Jesse Raphael how she would react if Phil was released: "I'd do what anyone in love would do. . . . But we only know each other three hours a week. We might not even like each other *in the real world.*" (Emphasis added.)

"Some marriages break down when the prisoner is released and both parties have difficulty adjusting to the changes they have undergone," wrote Tricia Hedin in a *Newsweek* article. Geraldine and Nathaniel Grimes, Jr., who married with so much optimism and enthusiasm in 1978 while he was doing life for murder, are now separated and planning to divorce. He was paroled on May 21, 1985, and according to his mother, the marriage lasted two years after that.

ENDINGS

Two stories now, about women who fell in love with killers. One has a happy ending. The other, with its grim and tragic finale, can serve as a cautionary tale. The first murderer killed his father but never went to prison for his crime. The second man spent seventeen years behind concrete and steel for murdering his mother and father, then was paroled. Both killers found women to love. One woman is still alive.

Fran, a registered nurse in Houston, Texas, always read the letters to the editor in *The Houston Post* and was rapidly becoming fascinated with one writer, David, an inmate serving a life sentence. "I was truly amazed at David's intelligence and articulate skills on almost every topic from classical music to women's rights." She decided she had to meet this man, and when she did, it was love at first sight. David, thirty-five, had been in prison for fourteen years for the 1969 murder of his mother and father. "He looked like a walking zombie. . . . It went right to my heart. . . . I knew this person had been terribly mistreated." Fran recognized a kindred spirit, another victim of soul murder.

David was an abused child and adolescent. When he was twenty-one and a senior in college, he and his father argued violently one night about U.S. involvement in Vietnam. David's father, who was mentally and physically brutal to both his wife and son, threatened to kill David for what he called un-American ideas. David's mother took her husband's side in the argument; she always did. Fran said David's mother was "pathologically adapted to her terrifying situation. Like so many women so afflicted, she would frequently assist in the violence against David as a means of identifying with her oppressor."

When the argument was over, David's parents went to bed. David hid. Hours later, he "emerged in a state of terror" and killed them both. Arrested, tried, and convicted, David was sentenced to life.

Fourteen years later, he met Fran. When she visited, David rarely smiled, never laughed. His was a "seemingly emotionless demeanor. He needed to be that way to survive." But Fran, rather than being discouraged by his lack of expression, tried to draw David out. She wanted to help him because she recognized his pain; it was a reflection of hers.

"Maybe it was the years of abuse that I had. A terrible life can either destroy you or make you a terrible person." What did it do to Fran?

When she was very little, her mother left her father and married another man. Fran's new "grandfather," her stepfather's father, sexually abused her when she was four. Throughout her childhood, she was beaten. "People thought that's how you raised kids: You beat the hell out of them."

When she was twelve, her mother, who had a history of psychiatric problems, committed suicide. Later, Fran went to live with her natural father, who "had sexual problems. He never tried to have intercourse with me but tried to do everything else. He didn't know the dividing line."

Sexually abused, battered, and beaten, Fran carried her burden alone through life until she met David many years later. "All the short circuits I had in life led me to the real thing," she says of their love. They met in 1983 and married in June 1984. For the next three years, Fran worked to get David released, convinced that he had murdered because of the abuse he'd suffered. He should "have been charged with the lesser offense of voluntary manslaughter and certainly not given a life sentence." Fran "played detective," talked to David's relatives to find out more about "the craziness of his parents," went on radio and television arguing on his behalf, persuaded *The Houston Post* to print an editorial, and appealed again and again to the state parole board. All of Fran's passion and sacrifice paid off; David was paroled on January 19, 1987.

Today, they are happily married and very productive. David is even able to show happiness. "Now, he's very expressive; he laughs. I say, 'David, you're laughing. That's wonderful.' " Despite the fact that Fran's sister and brother won't speak to her because of her relationship, and although she's had some problems with work because of their marriage, Fran is still firmly committed to David. He assists a social worker at a Houston hospital and is finishing a master's degree in psychology. She is working toward a master's degree in psychiatric nursing. They live with three poodles and four cats and are trying to adopt a child.

Fran's fantasy of rescuing David has come true. "I had saved David's life, so to speak, and given him opportunity in life." Fran refers to David as "my loving husband," and although they argue occasionally, the disagreements never escalate, never become violent. Is Fran afraid that David, having killed once, could kill again? "You would think I'd be a liar if I never did [think about it], and for the first year, yes, I did. But now, I don't know why, but no, I'm not afraid. . . . If I was ever afraid of David, I wouldn't be with him. . . . The great, overriding feeling I have had about him is his suffering."

LOVE KILLS

". . . If you stay around long enough, you discover what we have learned again. . . . Love also kills," wrote columnist Pete Hamill. Love killed JoAnn Breton on December 14, 1987.

Twenty-one years earlier, in 1966, Bobby Breton came home from a date knowing he was in big trouble. His father's drunken body was lying on the floor directly in front of the door so he'd have to shove it against the old man to get into the house. Bobby was scared because if the old man was that drunk, he might wake up and beat him to within an inch of his life.

That's what happened; the door opened and Bobby's father woke up. What are you doing? screamed the older man. He whipped his belt out of its loops and went after Bobby. Bobby's grandmother screamed also: Leave him alone! Leave him alone! But Breton, Sr., was beyond hearing. He hated his son, hated his life, hated his mother—just hated. And Bobby was going to pay. He pushed his mother out of the way and ran toward Bobby. Bobby was crying, What did I ever do to you? He picked up a knife from the counter and rushed toward his father as his father came at him. I hate you, I hate you, Bobby screamed over and over as he drove the knife into his father's body.

His father fell to the floor, his drunkenness, his age, his rage, no match for his son. Robert J. Breton, nineteen, had committed patricide.

"His father was mean to Robert all the time. . . . He was ready to hit [him] all the time," Eva Breton testified during her grandson's trial. Her son was abusive and spent all his money on liquor, but Robert was a quiet, obedient boy who helped support the family, she said. It was an open-and-shut case of self-defense, said Judge Leo Gaffney. He gave Breton a one-to-two-year suspended sentence and placed him on parole for two years. The young man never went to jail for killing his father.

For the next two decades, nothing more was heard from Robert J. Breton in his hometown of Waterbury, Connecticut. He worked, married, raised a family. In 1971, Robert and his wife, JoAnn, had a son whom they named Robert, Jr. A third generation of Robert Bretons.

Fifteen years went by. By 1986, Robert and JoAnn were living apart and a divorce was imminent. JoAnn, a clerical worker, filed for a restraining order barring Robert from the house, saying he had broken furniture, put a hole in a wall, fired a shot into the ceiling.

When the divorce became final, during the second week of December 1987, the Bretons' son, a high school junior, told a neighbor that his father had threatened to kill his mother and had pulled a knife on her.

It was two weeks before Christmas and Robert Breton was furious that JoAnn had locked him out of his own house. So what if he knocked her around once in a while? So what if he gambled, had a girlfriend, drank? So what if they would be divorced in a matter of days? It was still his house.

Breton walked up to the front door and banged on it; JoAnn had changed the lock. When she didn't answer, he broke the glass and turned the knob from inside. Then he ran up the familiar steps into the bedroom they used to share. She was in bed. He punched her in the face a few times, yelling, Why did you do this to me? I hate you, I hate you.

He ran down to the kitchen and grabbed a knife. By the time he got back upstairs, she was out of bed, trying to dial the phone. He plunged the knife into her body. She stopped moving, stopped crying out.

He heard a noise on the stairs. Breton ran out of the bedroom and saw his sixteen-year-old son running toward him. He stabbed his son in the neck and the boy pitched backward, falling down the stairs, blood spurting out of his severed artery.

This time there was no leniency in the courtroom for Robert J. Breton. On April 11, 1989, twenty-two years after he was given a suspended sentence for killing his father, he was sentenced to death for the murder of his wife and son. He is on death row at Somers State Correctional Institution waiting to die in Connecticut's electric chair.

"This was a vicious, brutal murder," said John Griffin, Waterbury's chief inspector of detectives.

Did it have to happen? Why did JoAnn marry Robert Breton knowing that he had committed patricide? Didn't she understand that her life, and the life of any children they would have, would always be at risk living with a man who was capable of stabbing to death his own father? Why didn't JoAnn realize the danger of marrying a man who had killed? Or did she?

According to Detective Griffin, JoAnn knew Robert had killed his father and chose to ignore it. "It was common knowledge around here that he had done that." He described JoAnn as "a nice girl. Anyone we talked to who had known her said she was a nice girl."

Like many women who love men who kill, JoAnn suffered a traumatic loss when she was very young. She was six when her parents divorced, and she never saw her father again. JoAnn was raised by her mother and stepfather.

JoAnn's marriage to Robert Breton was a rocky one. Said her mother, "It was an on-and-off marriage—we tried to help her as much as we could. He was breaking everything in the house. Who knows if he hit her. But you know what love can do. She loved him.

"She always told me: 'I'm not scared that he's going to hit me.' But she had no peace. He was always calling her, always going over to her house. She wanted the divorce; there were too many arguments and he was gambling in the end. She cried to us. . . . He had a girlfriend for a while; he didn't bother her then."

Since Robert never went to prison for killing his father, it was easy for JoAnn to deny his violent nature so she could love and marry him. We will never know what was in JoAnn's mind and heart on the day she married Robert. She is gone and buried and her reasons for loving a murderer are gone with her.

JoAnn Breton represents an unvoiced fear. Is this what eventually happens to women who love murderers—when their men are released from prison, when their phantom lovers become real? JoAnn, who once thought herself passionately in love with a killer, who was able to overlook and rationalize his crime, is herself a murder victim.

Beaten, stabbed, robbed of her life by her husband, her untold story dead with her, JoAnn Breton may serve as a warning to other women who live with fantasies of love.

Bibliography

BOOKS AND ARTICLES

Abbott, Jack Henry. *In the Belly of the Beast.* New York: Random House, 1982.

Abbott, Jack Henry, with Naomi Zack. *My Return.* Buffalo, New York: Prometheus Books, 1987.

Abrahamsen, David. *Confessions of Son of Sam.* New York: Columbia University Press, 1985.

American Psychiatric Association. *Diagnostic and Statistical Manual of Mental Disorders* (3rd ed., revised). Washington, D.C.: American Psychiatric Association, 1987.

Arizona Daily Star. Articles from 1974, 1975, 1987, and 1989.

Arizona Republic. Articles from 1974, 1983, and 1986.

Bello, Stephen. *Doing Life: The Extraordinary Saga of America's Greatest Jailhouse Lawyer.* New York: St. Martin's Press, 1986.

Benjamin, Jessica. *The Bonds of Love.* New York: Pantheon Books, 1989.

Bucks County Courier Times (Bucks County, Pa.). Articles from 1980, 1981, 1982, 1983, and 1985.

Cahill, Tim. *Buried Dreams: Inside the Mind of a Serial Killer.* New York: Bantam Books, 1986.

Caputi, Jane. *The Age of Sex Crime.* Bowling Green, Ohio: Bowling Green State University Popular Press, 1987.

Cassell, Carol B. *Swept Away.* New York: Simon and Schuster, 1984.

Cowan, Connell, and Melvyn Kinder. *Smart Women, Foolish Choices.* New York: Clarkson N. Potter, Inc., 1985.

Daily Republican (Waterbury, Conn.). "Robert Breton Found Stabbed to Death," Dec. 3, 1966; "Robert, 19, Held in Fatal Stabbing," Dec. 4, 1966; "Breton Gets Stay in Death of Father," Feb. 8, 1967; "Breton Gets Suspended Term in Stabbing," April 12, 1967; "Family, Friends Bid Farewell to Mother, Son, Slain in Quarrel," Dec. 19, 1987; "Murder Trial to Begin This Week," March 27, 1989; "Doctor Says Beating Preceded Fatal Stabbing," March 30, 1989; "Guilty of Murdering Ex-Wife, Son," April 12, 1989; "Friend Says Divorce Upset Breton," Sept. 28, 1989; "Psychologist Says Breton Is Mentally Ill," Sept. 29, 1989; "Sentenced to Die," Oct. 28, 1989.

Dalton, Emmett. *When the Daltons Rode.* Garden City, New York: Doubleday, Doran & Company, Inc., 1931.

Davidson, Joy. *The Agony of It All.* Los Angeles: Jeremy P. Tarcher, Inc., 1988.

Davis, Hal. "Author-Killer Grills Widow of His Victim." *New York Post* (June 14, 1990): p. 4.

Davison, Gerald C., and John M. Neale. *Abnormal Psychology.* New York: John Wiley & Sons, 1986.

"Death Row Inmate's Wife Sues for Chance to Have Killer's Baby." *Palm Beach Post* (Palm Beach, Fla.), March 8, 1990 (AP).

Dietz, Park Elliot. "Mass, Serial and Sensational Homicides." *Bulletin of New York Academy of Medicine* 62 (1986): 477–91.

Dietz, Park Elliot, Robert R. Hazelwood, and Janet Warren. "The Sexually Sadistic Criminal and His Offenses." *Bulletin of the American Academy of Psychiatry and the Law* (1990), Vol. 18, No. 2, pp. 163–178.

Faulkner, Joseph E., Jr. "Walls and Bridges: The Experience of Loss in Wives of Men Sentenced to Live in Prison." MSW thesis, Smith College School for Social Work, Northampton, Mass., 1989.

Fawkes, Sandy. *Killing Time.* New York: Taplinger Publishing Company, 1979.

Forward, Susan, and Joan Torres. *Men Who Hate Women & the Women Who Love Them.* New York: Bantam Books, 1986.

Goleman, Daniel. "Dangerous Delusions: When Fans Are a Threat." *The New York Times* (Oct. 31, 1989): p. C1.

Hamill, Pete. Untitled column. *New York Post* (March 28, 1990).

Hanley, Robert. "Paroled Killer Accused in Deaths of 11 Women in Rochester Area." *The New York Times* (Jan. 6, 1990).

――――. "Rochester Slaying Suspect: A Gift-Giver With a Rage." *The New York Times* (Jan. 13, 1990).

Hedin, Tricia. "My Husband Is in Prison." *Newsweek* (December 15, 1986).

Hennegan, Alison. Introduction in *Reader, I Murdered Him: Original Crime Stories by Women*. Edited by Jen Green. New York: St. Martin's Press, 1989.

Hilberry, Conrad. *Luke Karamazov*. Detroit: Wayne State University Press, 1987.

Hite, Shere. *Women & Love: A Cultural Revolution in Progress*. New York: St. Martin's Press, 1987.

Jenkins, Philip. "Serial Murder in England 1940–1985." *Journal of Criminal Justice* 16 (1988): pp. 1–15.

Johnson, Robert A. *We: Understanding the Psychology of Romantic Love*. New York: Harper and Row, 1985.

Kasl, Charlotte Davis. *Women, Sex and Addiction*. New York: Ticknor & Fields, 1989.

"Kirk's Guilty Plea Called 'Primarily to Help Mary.' " *The Knoxville News-Sentinel* (Knoxville, Tenn.), March 8, 1984.

Larsen, Richard W. *Ted Bundy: The Deliberate Stranger*. Englewood Cliffs, N.J.: Prentice Hall, 1980.

Levin, Jack, and James Alan Fox. *Mass Murder: America's Growing Menace*. New York: Plenum Press, 1985.

Leyton, Elliott. *Hunting Humans: Inside the Minds of Mass Murderers*. New York: Pocket Books, 1986.

Los Angeles Times. Articles from 1987 and 1988.

McClelland, C. Ivor, compiler. *They Call Him Mr. Gacy*. Brighton, Colo.: McClelland Associates, 1989.

Mailer, Norman. *The Executioner's Song*. Boston: Little, Brown & Co., 1979.

Michaud, Stephen G., and Hugh Aynesworth. *The Only Living Witness: A True Account of Homicidal Insanity.* New York: Linden Press/Simon and Schuster, 1983.

Money, John, Ph.D. *Lovemaps.* New York: Irvington Publishers, 1986.

―――. *Love and Love Sickness: The Science of Sex, Gender Difference, and Pair Bonding.* Baltimore: Johns Hopkins Univesity Press, 1980.

Morgan, Robin. *The Demon Lover: On the Sexuality of Terrorism.* New York: W.W. Norton, 1989.

Nash, Jay Robert. *Bloodletters and Badmen: A Narrative Encyclopedia of American Criminals From the Pilgrims to the Present.* New York: M. Evans, 1973.

Norris, Joel. *Serial Killers: The Growing Menace.* New York: Doubleday, 1988.

Norwood, Robin. *Women Who Love Too Much.* New York: Pocket Books, 1986.

O'Brien, Darcy. *Two of a Kind: The Hillside Stranglers.* New York: New American Library, 1985.

Perlman, Shirley E. "Pikul's New Wife Says She Married for Love, Children." *Newsday* (Sept. 29, 1988).

―――. "Wife's Tale Has Court in Uproar." *Newsday* (Sept. 15, 1988).

Person, Ethel S. *Dreams of Love and Fateful Encounters: The Power of Romantic Passion.* New York: W.W. Norton, 1988.

Phoenix Gazette. Articles from 1974, 1983, 1984, and 1985.

Pileggi, Nicholas. "The Strange Case of Joseph Pikul." *New York* magazine (March 14, 1988).

"A Portrait of the Other Side of Success." *Newsday* (Oct. 31, 1988).

Rocky Mountain News (Denver). Articles from 1987 and 1989.

Rule, Ann. *The Stranger Beside Me.* New York: W.W. Norton & Co., 1980.

Schaef, Anne Wilson. *Escape From Intimacy: Untangling the Love Addictions.* San Francisco: Harper & Row, 1989.

Schaeffer, Brenda. *Is It Love or Is It Addiction?* New York: Harper & Row, 1988.

Schanberg, Sydney H. "Troubling Worries Over Pikul's Children." *Newsday* (May 13, 1988).

Segal, Jonathan. "Erotomania Revisited: From Krapelin to DSM-III-R." *The American Journal of Psychiatry* 146 (October 1989): 1261–66.

Senelick, Laurence. *The Prestige of Evil: The Murderer as Romantic Hero from Sade to Lacenaire.* New York: Garland Publishing, 1987.

Shengold, Leonard. *Soul Murder: The Effects of Childhood Abuse and Deprivation.* New Haven: Yale University Press, 1989.

Silence, Michael, and Jim Balloch. "Brushy Inmate, Lawyer at Large; Escape Car Found." *The Knoxville News-Sentinel* (April 2, 1983): p. 1.

Sternberg, Robert J., and Michael L. Barnes, eds. *The Psychology of Love.* New Haven: Yale University Press, 1988.

Sullivan, Ronald. "Author Facing Damages for Murder." *The New York Times* (June 6, 1990): p. B2.

———. "Author Is Told to Pay Millions for '81 Slaying." *The New York Times* (June 16, 1990).

Tanay, Emanuel, with Lucy Freeman. *The Murderers.* Indianapolis: Bobbs Merrill, 1976.

Tennov, Dorothy. *Love and Limerence.* New York: Stein and Day, 1979.

Terry, Maury. *The Ultimate Evil.* Garden City, New York: Doubleday & Company, 1987.

Times-Picayune (New Orleans). Articles from 1986, 1987, and 1989.

Trantino, Tommy. *Lock the Lock.* New York: Knopf, 1968.

Weller, Sheila. "In Their Best Interest." *Ms.* magazine (July 1988).

Westword, Denver's News & Arts Weekly (1984).

"Why Women Marry Men in Prison." *Ebony* magazine (June 1983): p. 150.

"Wife-Killer Joseph Pikul Died of AIDS." *Daily Freeman* (Kingston, N.Y.), July 16, 1989 (AP).

Wilson, Colin. *A Criminal History of Mankind*. New York: Putnam Publishing Group, 1984.

Wolfe, Linda. *Wasted: The Preppie Murder*. New York: Simon and Schuster, 1989.

"Woman Lawyer Aids Escape." *The Knoxville News-Sentinel* (Knoxville, Tenn.), April 1983.

Yancey, Matt. Article on Anna Sandhu and James Earl Ray, supplementary material, from The Associated Press and The New York Times News Service (Oct. 14, 1978).

TELEVISION PROGRAMS

"A Current Affair" syndicated television program. Segments on Robert Chambers: Aug. 28, 1986; Sept. 11, 1986; Nov. 13, 1986; Feb. 8, 1988; May 16, 1988; May 17, 1988; and Sept. 25, 1989.

"A Current Affair" syndicated television program. Segments on Joseph Pikul and Mary Bain Pikul: Sept. 11, 1988; Sept. 15, 1988; Sept. 19, 1988; Sept. 20, 1988; Sept. 21, 1988; Jan. 31, 1989; March 20, 1989; and June 7, 1990.

Geraldo Rivera syndicated television program: "Wives of Death Row" (January 18, 1990); "People Who Should Never Get Out of Prison" (November 13, 1989); and "The Jailhouse Romance" (August 26, 1988).

"Hard Copy" segment on marriage of Hillside Strangler Kenneth Bianchi: "The Woman and the Strangler" (December 7, 1989).

Morton Downey syndicated television program: "Women Who Love Killers" (May 1988).

"People Are Talking" syndicated television program: "A Woman Outside in Love with a Man Inside" (March 22, 1988).

"The Reporters" segment: "Prisoner of Love" (Sept. 9, 1989).

Sally Jesse Raphael syndicated television program: "Forbidden Love" (April 26, 1989) and "Prison Love" (June 21, 1990).